MATROLOGY

MATROLOGY

A BIBLIOGRAPHY OF WRITINGS
BY CHRISTIAN WOMEN FROM THE FIRST
TO THE FIFTEENTH CENTURIES

Andrew Kadel

CONTINUUM • NEW YORK

1995

The Continuum Publishing Company
370 Lexington Avenue, New York, NY 10017

Library of Congress Cataloging-in-Publication Data

Kadel, Andrew.
    Matrology : a bibliography of writings by Christian women from the
first to the fifteenth centuries / Andrew Kadel.
        p.   cm.
    Includes bibliographical references and indexes.
    ISBN 0-8264-0676-9 (hardcover : alk. paper)
    1. Christian literature—Bibliography.   2. Christian literature,
Early—Bibliography.   3. Christian women—Bibliography.   4. Women
authors—Bibliography.   I. Title.
Z7751.K33   1994
[BR117]
016.27′0082–dc20   94–30157
                                                                    CIP

Contents

5

Appendix

Acknowledgments

The work for this book was done almost entirely at the Burke Library of Union Theological Seminary in New York, with occasional forays to the Butler Library of Columbia University. I wish to thank Dr. Milton McC. Gatch, the director of the Burke Library, and the rest of my colleagues there for support and the resources to bring this project to completion. Many colleagues at the library as well as students and faculty helped by calling resources to my attention and assisting me in thinking out problems in this book. Michael Bereza in particular screened new materials coming into the library for things relevant to the women and their writings of the period covered here. I especially want to acknowledge and thank my colleague and mentor, Seth Kasten, without whose encouragement and constructive criticism this book would not have gone forward.

While I received assistance from many quarters, I was particularly gratified by the friendly assistance provided by scholars working in languages of the eastern Mediterranean, which are frequently outside the knowledge of scholars of European thought and literature, specifically: Coptic, Armenian, and Greek. Professor Deirdre Good of General Theological Seminary was very helpful when I was lost among the conflicting claims in the anonymous and pseudonymous world of the gnostics. Professor Peter Cowie of Columbia University brought the Armenian hymnographers to my attention and was kind enough to locate the sources for me. Eva Catafygiotu Topping responded to my letters with much very helpful information about Byzantine women authors.

A work such as this is necessarily derivative. Every editor and

13

author who is cited has made a contribution to the book. Very often those contributions go much further than is readily apparent. I would be very remiss if I did not make special mention of the work of Peter Dronke. His *Women Writers of the Middle Ages* is widely recognized for careful and scholarly analysis of women's texts from the third to the fourteenth centuries and sensitive observations about the self-expression of women in this period. I owe a particular debt, however, to Dr. Dronke's bibliography in the back of that book, which contains a checklist of women's writings in their most scholarly editions. The fact that this list was really only usable for those comfortable reading in Latin convinced me to go ahead with this book.

The responsibility for using all this help well lies of course with me. I have made all judgments regarding inclusion or exclusion, the accuracy of citations, and whether books indeed contain works of a given author.

Finally, this book is dedicated to my daughters, Elisabeth, Rachel, and Magdalen, who have always managed to express themselves in their own strong and independent voices.

Introduction

This book is a reply to a difficult reference question. The graduate assistant for an introductory Old Testament class came to me with a question about the history of interpretation: "We are teaching the students to look at what Jerome and Augustine had to say about their assigned passages, but a lot of women in the class are asking what women had to say. Which women wrote about the Old Testament?" A reasonable question, but there was no reference book available dealing with ancient and medieval times that enumerated women authors at all, let alone which ones wrote about scripture. Investigation indicated that there are a lot of questions about texts by women and about comparison of texts by the gender of their authors that need a systematic tool in order to be fully answered. The title, *Matrology*, could be loosely rendered from Greek as "words of the mothers." It is in contrast to a number of major reference works called "Patrologies." In the nineteenth century, Jacques-Paul Migne compiled tremendous sets of Christian texts (nearly four hundred huge volumes) that he entitled *Patrologia latina* and *Patrologia graeca*, and in the twentieth century Berthold Altaner and Johannes Quasten compiled large bibliographical works, each of which is entitled *Patrology*. The goals of this book are much more modest. First, the number of authors and the length of texts are much smaller. All the texts represented in this book taken together would be substantially shorter than a comparable edition of the works of Saint Augustine. Second, the audience for and interest in these texts are much more interdisciplinary and diverse than those envisioned by the patrologists. Rather than compile detailed biographical and technical information about authors and texts, this intends to be a usable guide for nonspecialists who may be unacquainted with the complex abbreviations and terminology of medieval and early Christian studies while maintaining enough information for scholars of all sorts to gain access to exact original texts and technical discussions of them. The past decade or so has seen a boom in publication of translations and editions of texts by women. *Matrology* is intended to enable anyone to get hold of these writings, most of which are much more available than most people realize. Anthologies such as those by Elizabeth Petroff, Katharina Wilson, Ross Shepard Kraemer, Serinity Young, and others that are referred to in this book are available at most college and many public libraries. Many of the anthologies and English translations are available in paperback editions from booksellers or publishers. Reading the actual words of women from other times is bound to give new perspective on the understanding of that past and new insight into our situation today.

Scope

The goal of this book is to list every Christian woman who wrote before 1500 c.e. and her writings that have appeared in print since 1800. An appendix contains references to some works that are known to survive but that are only in manuscript form or in rare printed editions from the fifteenth through the eighteenth century. There are bound to be omissions, either from error or from new texts coming to light and being published in accessible editions. The author would be glad to know of corrections or additional material that might be incorporated into a later edition of this book.

Since the body of writings by women is so small, I have chosen to err on the side of inclusiveness in virtually all cases. The term *Christian women* includes all women who would have regarded themselves as Christian, whether their writings are religious or not, whether they were regarded by the church as orthodox or heretical, whether they were from Asia, Africa, or Europe. It is hoped that readers will make use of this for purposes beyond what the author can envision or program. Christianity is chosen as a unifying factor for this book because the development of Christianity had a tremendous and quite distinct impact on ancient civilization in Europe, Northern Africa, and the Middle East and in many ways formed medieval European and Byzantine culture. The separation of interest between religion, politics, home life and child rearing that is usually assumed today is foreign to both antiquity and the Middle Ages. No judgment is made about which texts are significant, useful, acceptable, or appropriate, only that they can be attributed to Christian women.

The decision to include only Christian women demarcated the beginning of the period that this bibliography covers. Jewish and Hellenistic texts, no matter how influential, could not have been the product of Christianity. The coverage ends with 1500. There are a number of reasons for this, not the least of which is that sixteenth-century studies is a distinct historical subdiscipline with its own complex research problems, and there are bibliographic tools beginning with 1500. In addition, none of the authors included here is likely to have thought of her writings being printed. Publication was a very different process in the Middle Ages (see Elizabeth Eisenstein, *The Printing Press as an Agent of Change* [Cambridge University Press, 1979]). When printing, which was first used commercially in the 1450s, reached maturity around the turn of the century, the number and type of texts from all sources increased dramatically. The increase in literacy and better preservation of manuscripts have made it difficult to be sure that all extant fifteenth-century writings are accounted for in this bibliography. To have included the sixteenth century would have required an entirely different approach.

This work is intended to be useful to the broadest possible audience, undergraduates and general readers as well as scholars in a number of different disciplines. Materials that would be usable only by specialists, such as manuscripts and rare books, are not included. Generally the original-language editions will give more detailed guidance to these materials. Historical scholarship and the publication of ancient and medieval materials boomed in the late nineteenth century. Many of the editions from this period are still heavily cited in literature, and frequently the only or best edition of a work will have been published during this period. Books from before this period are less available and often kept in library rare book departments. Thus the publication dates included are 1800 to early 1994. No authors or works are included unless the texts are known to still exist. As stated above, there is an appendix that includes those works that exist only in the form of manuscript or rare book.

Structure

The entries are arranged in groups that have a variety of relations to one another. These groupings may be by genre, language, social background, or organizational setting, and they fall in roughly chronological order. Indexes at the back of the book provide a strict chronological order and alphabetical listing of the authors. Each entry begins with a brief description of the author or authors it contains. After this, some entries contain one or more citations to secondary works, that is, *about* the author or her works, or a bibliography or a general but relevant discussion of a genre, time period, or group of people. These are given only when they will help to illuminate the authorship of a work and its background or to refer the reader to important bibliography about the author. Often, no secondary work is listed, since the introductory material and bibliographies of most of the translations, selections, and editions provide appropriate guidance.

The main bibliography follows, grouped by language. English editions of the full text are always listed first, if they are available. As with most other lists in the bibliography, the order of entries within the list of English translations is reverse chronological by publication date. In general, a newer edition will be more readily available and more up-to-date in terms of scholarship. This is not meant to imply that the newer text or translation is necessarily the best, but simply more available. In one or two instances, strict chronological order has been violated because one translation is substantially more widespread than another that might be newer. The English translations are followed by a list of selections, which, unless otherwise specified, are found in anthologies listed in the Anthologies Cited bibliography located after this introduction. These selections are listed in alphabetical order by the translator of the selection. The full bibliographical citations for the anthologies appear in Anthologies Cited. In a couple of cases where several anthologies of selections from a single author have been published, there are two separately labeled sections of selections. Most of these selections are in English although there are a small number in German or French. These are followed by a list of "critical editions." This is a technical term for an edition that preserves all available textual evidence in detailed notes. A good critical edition will enable a scholar to determine what variations are present in each manuscript as well as in early translations and early printed editions. Such editions contain critical introductions about the text and its author as well as other information the editor deems important. Sometimes there is more than one critical edition, and sometimes there is none. The list of critical editions may be followed by a list of other editions in the original languages (these editions are not by uncritical editors, but they do not concentrate on the textual apparatus). Translations into other languages follow the original. These may be important for their introductory material and bibliography as well as useful for those who have more difficulty with Greek or Latin than with German or French.

At the end of the book is a bibliography of secondary sources. Except for the bibliography of bibliographies, this is a very brief selection of books in English of a more general nature. They are included because they are either established and essential works or recent studies. The purpose of this final bibliography is to aid further exploration of women and their writings in antiquity and the Middle Ages; it is not intended in any way to be complete or authoritative.

Women and Writing in Antiquity and the Middle Ages

There are nearly 250 names of women authors included in this book. That is more than I expected at the outset, and it is more than most scholars would have projected. But when one considers that a large number of these are represented by a single text of less than a page and that this is the total available output from fifteen centuries, it is still surprising how few texts survive from women. Some manuscripts certainly perished through the ravages of time or warfare or inquisition. When few copies existed, the works would be lost. It is possible and even likely that more texts will be discovered, either among unpublished manuscripts of the Middle Ages or among published works attributed to "Anonymous." This latter possibility is particularly likely among medieval hagiographical works, especially those depicting the lives of women. However, it is also an unavoidable fact that few texts survive because relatively few were composed by women in antiquity and the Middle Ages. Education was a rare and costly commodity. In the Roman Empire, the sons of the aristocracy received instruction, and some slaves were skilled in reading and writing either because they were educated before enslavement or because it was useful for their masters to have a secretary or notary. It was seldom deemed useful to have women learn to read and write since these were not necessary in normal domestic duties. Some of the aristocracy, however, allowed their daughters to learn to read and write. Most of the authors in both antiquity and the Middle Ages came from the upper social and economic classes. In addition to the scarcity of literacy, writing materials were expensive and the leisure to compose and write was difficult to come by.

There is no reason to doubt that the texts that we have could actually have been written down by the women who composed them. With few exceptions, the upper-class connections of the authors are unmistakable, and there was no taboo on women learning to write if they had the opportunity. However, it was customary for certain types of correspondence to be taken to a notary for drafting, even when the sender was literate. The distinction between thoroughgoing composition of a text, dictation, and the paraphrase of a secretary or notary is not always completely clear. In this work, all three of these are included if the substantial content can be attributed to a female author. Thus the *Martyrdom of Perpetua* appears in places to be in Perpetua's own very personal words; the work, however, also contains a description of her death in the arena, a description that must have been composed by someone else. The texts of Saint Macrina are unequivocally by her brother, Gregory, but contain speeches that may well be in substance from Macrina. There are official letters from members of the imperial household. Certainly, someone like Pulcheria could have afforded an amanuensis capable of elegant composition or editing, yet did she use one? That is for the reader to decide.

As Christianity became more established and the Roman Empire deteriorated, monasticism became increasingly the center of European literacy. Because the monastic establishments were segregated by sex, there was often the opportunity for increased literacy among the nuns. In the High Middle Ages, there were even a large number of scriptoria in convents, and many nuns became skilled copyists and illuminators of manuscripts. The sisters involved in these pursuits had taken vows of poverty, but they were usually also choir nuns whose families had paid substantial dowries upon their admission to the convent. All in all, the reader should be aware that literacy was for those who could afford it.

Literacy is one thing; preparation to teach and write theology, philosophy, or literature is something else again. Before the Renaissance, there is almost a complete lack of what might be called systematic writing by women. There are visions, letters, poetry (usually brief lyrics, with the notable exception of Proba's *Cento*), but there are no systematic expositions of the books of the Bible, the doctrines of Christian theology, law, or the philosophy of the ancients except for a couple of brief works by Hildegard of Bingen that she composed to teach the nuns of her convent. Even her major works were reports of visions and prophecies. Why was this? There are different ways in which this has been evaluated. The purpose of compiling all these texts is to let each reader come to her or his own conclusion with complete enough data. It is possible that the more affective mode of visions is better suited to the feminine psyche; it is also possible that women had no opportunity to enter the arena of discourse except through the oblique route of relating special revelations from God. It is certainly true that women were not allowed to preach or speak publicly outside their convents, unless they were people of truly outstanding audacity and courage. Fortunately, we do have the writings of a few of these.

Hagiography

One of the most common impulses among religious people is to recount the stories of holy people. This is particularly strong among Christians, who developed their distinct identity and eventual power in the Roman Empire from the stories of the martyrs who sacrificed their lives rather than compromise their convictions. One could even argue that much of the New Testament is hagiographical and martyrological in nature. It is no surprise, then, that hagiography (Gr: *hagios* = holy one + *graphos* = written) predominates among the texts of Christian women, even beyond visionary literature. The stories of holy women were as important as the stories of holy men, and because women were neither called upon nor given the opportunity to participate in the theoretical and systematic exposition of the Christian faith, or in its formal governance, hagiography stands out even more for women than it does for men.

It should be remembered that lives of saints and other hagiographical texts are always *religious texts*. The purpose of Christian hagiography is to show how God's saving activity is manifested in the lives of concrete individuals. Many sources may be used: eyewitnesses, the writings of the individual, court documents, oral traditions, biographies, writings regarding lives of other saints, and so on; but the purpose is to bear testimony to the way in which God is revealed. One should not expect such a testimony to convey its sources unaltered or to address the concerns that modern historians and biographers might have. It is clear that the perspective of the person who is writing the story of the saint will determine the way the story is told and its contents. Sometimes the hagiographer will have known the saint or will have access to firsthand reminiscences of her friends. At other times, centuries of legends intervene between the saint and the writer. Some hagiographers use sources to build a portrait of a unique individual, while others have a preconceived idea of the life and behavior of a saint and use biographical information to demonstrate how this saint fits that pattern.

Hagiography occurs in this bibliography in three types of cases. The first is when the sources of the hagiographer are close enough to make it possible to discern the actual voice of the saint in the text. The *Passion of Perpetua* and the *Life of Macrina* are examples of this. The second case is when the hagiographer is a woman, so that the life of the saint itself is a woman's writing. Hugeberg of Heidenheim's work on Saint Willibald, Sergia's *Narration concerning Olympias,* or the writings of Clemence of Barking regarding Saint Catherine of Alexandria are three different types of this. The third case is when the writing may have been done by a man, but he directly used the testimonies of women, usually the religious community of the saint, which can be discerned through careful reading. The best examples of this are the lives of the Beguine saints by Thomas Cantimpré.

The authorship of works from antiquity and especially the Middle Ages is often more attributable to religious communities than to individuals, even when the name of an individual may be attached. The Dominican convent chronicles are clear examples of this, and the role of community is equally important at Helfta, where Gertrude the Great helped Mechthild of Hackeborn to edit and write her work, and at Rupertsberg, where the astounding illuminated manuscript of Hildegard of Bingen's *Scivias* may have been produced in her convent's scriptorium.

Monasticism

Monasticism developed in Christianity as a response to changes in the Roman Empire and the church with individuals going into the desert to seek both greater individual holiness and the renewal of faith in the church. Women were involved in this from early on, as evidenced by the sayings of the Desert Mothers. Communities for women and for men and women in various types of shared or parallel organizations certainly existed from the fourth century onward. Asceticism was always an important element in Christian monasticism, but the aspects of sexual continence, celibacy, and virginity soon became particularly important. This led to progressively stricter segregation between men and women monastics. In some respects, this led to greater independence for the convents, and in most matters they became self-sufficient. However, the sacraments had to be administered by a male priest. The women's communities were thus more subservient in theological matters than they were in practical matters. Thus no texts survive from Hilda of Whitby, who presided over a double monastery in England that was the site of the synod that united Roman and Celtic Catholicism in the seventh century. The practical politics of a mediator were more acceptable from a woman than the theological interpretation of them would have been. The texts that survive from these convents are either hagiography or reports of visions, revelations, or prophecies that the (male) spiritual directors/confessors of the nuns decided should be written down and preserved. The emphasis on virginity also led to the development of ideals that helped monastic communities to grow and also influenced the ways in which the lives of devout young women developed. By the late Middle Ages, typical descriptions of women saints state their opposition to marriage from an early age (if the woman had been married, it was often stated that it was against her will), and a large number of the most admired women saints bore the stigmata (wounds of Christ on hands, feet, and/or side) and otherwise suffered long-term illness. Accounts of mystical experience, including imagery of betrothal to Christ, figure prominently in the medieval ideal of a holy woman.

Most of the monasticism of Western Europe is traceable to the tradition of the Benedictines until the thirteenth century. Those religious who were not strictly Benedictine were usually closely associated with the order; for instance, the Cistercians were a movement to reform Benedictine monasticism to a more primitive strictness. In the late twelfth and thirteenth centuries, popular movements in favor of "apostolic simplicity" and embracing the ideal of voluntary radical poverty led to the formation of the mendicant orders, the Franciscans and Dominicans. At about the same time that these orders were being established in Italy and

Spain, the Beguines arose in Belgium and Holland. Unlike the mendicant orders, the Beguines and their male counterparts, the Beghards, were never formally organized or recognized by the church. The ideal of radical poverty and simplicity motivated the early Beguines as much as it did the early Franciscans. But while Francis and Clare established strictly enclosed convents for the Poor Clares, as the Franciscan nuns are called, the Beguines lived a life much more in the world, running schools and working with the sick. Since they were not an official order, Beguines took no formal vows and were free to decide to leave to get married. Because unmarried women outnumbered unmarried men in thirteenth-century Europe (the result of wars and the popularity of religious orders for men) and because the dowry required for entrance into a convent was often beyond the means of the families of many unattached women, joining the Beguines was an alternative that was pursued by a great many women at this time. There were similar movements of women throughout the continent of Europe. The freedom of the Beguines meant that their communities were not uniform either in practice or in belief. Church officials worried that the Beguines would be influenced by heretics such as the Albigensians. Thus measures were enacted to pressure Beguines to join or affiliate with established religious orders such as the Franciscans, Dominicans, or Cistercians. By the beginning of the fourteenth century the beguinages lost their influence or were incorporated into religious orders, most notably the Dominicans, although a few independent beguinages survived in Holland as late as the eighteenth century. Some Beguines who insisted on remaining independent of ecclesiastical control were punished as heretics. We are fortunate that Marguerite Porete's work was preserved in anonymous manuscripts after she and her book were burned at the stake.

Heretics

When one examines the works of people such as Marguerite Porete or Joan of Arc, who were burned as heretics, one later venerated as a saint and the other discovered and appreciated only by twentieth-century scholarship, it becomes apparent that the judgment of whether a person or her opinions are inside or outside the accepted scope of the Christian church depends on a number of factors that may not stand the test of time within the church or be relevant to the interests of those who are interested in Christian culture from outside the official church. In this book the widest definition of "Christian" has been used in including authors. In many respects, the difference between "orthodox" and "heretical" can often be explained more easily by social factors than by differences in belief. Just about the only voices of women born poor are among the "heretics" — Joan of Arc, the Catharist heretics whose testimony was preserved by the inquisitor Jacques Fournier, and some of the Beguines. It is hard to establish the exact social situation of gnostics represented in the materials from Nag Hammadi, or the communities that produced the apocryphal Acts of the Apostles, but this context is important for understanding the significance of the differences of opinion that later were called orthodoxy and heresy. This book contains citations for non-Christian poets in medieval Iceland because these texts shed a very interesting light on the social and spiritual impact of the arrival of Christianity in Iceland, particularly with regard to the place of women in religion and literature.

Not all Christian women were celibate, although the technical term *religious* refers to a consecrated celibate. Some of the most revealing texts come from mothers such as Perpetua and Dhuoda, and the latter's entire book comes from her concern for her absent son. Christine de Pisan took up a career as a professional writer precisely because she had to support her children after the death of her husband. While texts such as Dhuoda's and Christine's do not have the exclusively "religious" concerns of those produced by nuns and beguines, it is striking how naturally Christian piety, values, and beliefs play a central role in their thought and expression. A complete picture of women in Christianity is not possible if one focuses only on the religious virtuosos and leaves out the mothers, lovers, and singers whose experience is equally Christian.

By the late Middle Ages, literacy increased tremendously. This is the time that is often identified as the early portion of the Renaissance. I have included some collections of letters and other minor texts from this period, but I am confident that there are many more letters and such extant either in manuscript form or published among the letters of men or in editions that are not readily available. By the fifteenth century, the detailed enumeration of every woman's writings may not be feasible. Yet the greater number of texts such as we find among the Paston letters enables a much more detailed insight into the life of the times.

A tool such as this is valuable only if its users have more and different ideas of its use than its author does. It is my intention to leave as many alternatives as possible for the interpretation and evaluation of these texts. Less experienced readers should proceed with caution, here as well as elsewhere in these matters. The judgments of the compiler of a bibliography, the editor of an anthology, or the translator or editor of a full text about whether a work is in fact by a certain person, or a person of a given gender, or even by a person of a given set of opinions, is open to much debate. Some entries are included here even though it is doubtful that the author is a woman (a good example is the very first entry — the Epistle to the Hebrews). Some authors, even well-respected ones, bend the meaning of texts to fit a thesis. Critical reading and independent evaluation of the actual texts are essential, even if that means disagreeing with experts or abandoning a theory that is attractive but not borne out by the words of the authors. It is important to appreciate the voices of women, both because their intrinsic value has not been fully appreciated and because all of humanity will be better understood when every facet of it is fully appreciated.

Anthologies (and Other Selections of Texts) Cited in This Work

Bowie, Fiona, ed., and Oliver Davies, trans. *Beguine Spirituality: Mystical Writings of Mechthild of Magdeburg, Beatrice of Nazareth, and Hadewijch of Brabant.* New York: Crossroad, 1990.

Campbell, Karen J., ed. *German Mystical Writings.* New York: Continuum, 1991 (German Library 5).

Clark, Elizabeth A., trans. *Women in the Early Church.* Wilmington, Del.: Glazier, 1983; reprint, Collegeville, Minn.: Liturgical Press, 1990 (Message of the Fathers of the Church 13).

Colledge, Edmund, trans. *Mediaeval Netherlands Religious Literature.* Leiden and New York: Sythoff; London: House and Maxwell, 1965 (Bibliotheca Neerlandica). Includes the original Dutch of Beatrice, a Middle Dutch legend.

Dronke, Peter. *Women Writers of the Middle Ages: A Critical Study of Texts from Perpetua (d. 203) to Marguerite Porete (d. 1310).* Cambridge and New York: Cambridge University Press, 1984.

Hirshfield, Jane, ed. *Women in Praise of the Sacred: Forty-three Centuries of Spiritual Poetry by Women.* New York: HarperCollins, 1994.

Homeyer, Helene, trans. *Dichterinnen des Altertums und des frühen Mittelalters: Zweisprachige textausgabe.* Paderborn: Schöningh, 1979.

Kraemer, Ross Shepard, ed. *Maenads, Martyrs, Matrons, Monastics: A Sourcebook on Women's Religions in the Greco-Roman World.* Philadelphia: Fortress, 1988.

MacHaffie, Barbara J., ed. *Readings in Her Story: Women in Christian Tradition.* Minneapolis, Minn.: Fortress, 1992.

Oden, Amy G., ed. *In Her Words: Women's Writings in the History of Christian Thought.* Nashville: Abingdon, 1994.

Oehl, Wilhelm, ed. *Deutsche Mystikerbriefe des Mittelalters: 1100– 1550.* Munich: Georg Müller, 1931.

Petroff, Elizabeth, ed. *Medieval Women's Visionary Literature.* New York: Oxford University Press, 1986.

Thiébaux, Marcelle, trans. *The Writings of Medieval Women.* New York: Garland, 1987 (Garland Library of Medieval Literature 14); 2d ed.: New York: Garland, 1994 (Garland Library of Medieval Literature 100; series B).

Wilson, Katharina M., ed. *Medieval Women Writers.* Athens: University of Georgia Press, 1984.

———. *Women Writers of the Renaissance and Reformation.* Athens: University of Georgia Press, 1987.

Wilson-Kastner, Patricia, ed. *A Lost Tradition: Women Writers of the Early Church.* Washington, D.C.: University Press of America, 1981.

Wright, J. Robert, ed. *Readings for the Daily Office from the Early Church.* New York: Church Hymnal Corp., 1991. Includes author, topical, and theological indexes.

Young, Serinity, ed. *An Anthology of Sacred Texts by and about Women.* New York: Crossroad, 1993.

Zum Brunn, Emilie, and Georgette Epiney-Burgard, eds. *Women Mystics in Medieval Europe.* 1st American ed. New York: Paragon, 1989. Translation of *Femmes troubadours de Dieu.*

Chapter 1

The Earliest Writings
of Christian Women

New Testament and New Testament Apocrypha

Epistle to the Hebrews

The nineteenth book of the New Testament gives only very slight internal evidence of the identity of its author. This has led to a great deal of speculation about who may have written it. The great German church historian Adolf von Harnack advanced the theory that Hebrews may have been written by Priscilla, known to be an acquaintance of Paul and Apollos. J. M. Ford suggested that the author may have been Mary, the mother of Jesus. While there has been some discussion of the Priscilla theory, neither has received much acceptance among scholars. In fact, no theory that names a specific person as the author of this book has been widely adopted. Some essential sources for these arguments are listed below.

Ford, J. Massynbyrde. "The Mother of Jesus and the Authorship of the Epistle to the Hebrews." *The Bible Today* 82 (1976) pp. 683–94.

Harnack, Adolf von. "Probabilia über die Adresse und den Verfasser des Hebräerbriefs." *Zeitschrift für die Neutestamentliche Wissenschaft* 1 (1900) pp. 16–41.

Hoppin, R. *Priscilla: Author of the Epistle to the Hebrews, and Other Essays.* New York: Exposition, 1969.

Apocryphal Acts of the Apostles

Beyond the canonical material found in the New Testament, there is a substantial literature that tells about Jesus and the people surrounding him that, for various reasons, did not become part of the New Testament. Most of these Acts and Gospels are written pseudonymously, claiming to be written by an authoritative person from the past. It is impossible to be certain of the authorship of this material. This is complicated by the fact that most of these do not survive intact, but only in fragments. There have been theories that some of the apocryphal Acts of the Apostles may have been written by women. The two listed here are the most prominent candidates. The *Acts of Paul* is a long, loosely organized collection of stories about Paul the apostle. In one section that sometimes circulated separately, the *Acts of Paul and Thecla,* a woman (Thekla/Thecla) is portrayed as preaching. The *Acts of John* is usually considered to be a gnostic work. The reasons for considering the possibility that it was written by a woman are the prominent position that women play in the narrative and the scandalous reputation that the gnostics possessed for having women preach. Below are a few citations related to the ongoing discussion of these questions.

SECONDARY SOURCES

Davies, Stevan L. *The Revolt of the Widows: The Social World of the Apocryphal Acts.* Carbondale: Southern Illinois University Press; London: Feffer and Simons, 1980.

MacDonald, Dennis Ronald. *The Legend and the Apostle: The Battle for Paul in Story and Canon.* Philadelphia: Westminster, 1983.

———. "The Role of Women in the Production of the Apocryphal Acts of Apostles." *Iliff Review 41* (1984) pp. 21–38. Debate with Stevan L. Davies.

COLLECTIONS (ENGLISH)

Schneemelcher, Wilhelm, ed., and R. McL. Wilson, trans. *New Testament Apocrypha.* 2 vols. Rev. ed. Cambridge: Lutterworth; Louisville: Westminster/John Knox, 1991–93. Translation of *Neutestamentliche Apokryphen.* The Apocryphal Acts are in vol. 2.

Hennecke, Edgar, and Wilhelm Schneemelcher, eds., R. McL. Wilson, trans. *New Testament Apocrypha*. 2 vols. Philadelphia: Westminster, 1963–65. Translation of *Neutestamentliche Apokryphen*, ed. Edgar Hennecke.

Elliot, James K., ed. *The Apocryphal New Testament: A Collection of Apocryphal Christian Literature in English Translation*. Oxford: Clarendon; New York: Oxford University Press, 1993. A revision and new translation of M. R. James's *The Apocryphal New Testament*.

James, Montague Rhodes, ed. *The Apocryphal New Testament: Being the Apocryphal Gospels, Acts, Epistles, and Apocalypses, with Other Narratives and Fragments*. Corrected ed. Oxford: Clarendon, 1953.

Acts of Paul

ENGLISH

"Acts of Paul and Thecla." In Elizabeth A. Clark, trans., *Women in the Early Church*, pp. 78–88.

Roberts, Alexander, and James Donaldson, eds. "Thecla, *Acts of Paul and Thecla*." In Amy G. Oden, ed., *In Her Words: Women's Writings in the History of Christian Thought*, pp. 21–25.

———. "Acts of Paul and Thecla." In *Ante-Nicene Fathers*. Reprint, Grand Rapids: Eerdmans, 1951, 8:487–92.

See also Hennecke, Schneemelcher, Elliot, and James, above.

ENGLISH AND COPTIC

Goodspeed, Edgar Johnson, ed. *The Book of Thekla*. Chicago: University of Chicago Press, 1901 (Historical and Linguistic Studies in Literature related to the New Testament, 1st ser., texts vol. 1, pt. 1; Ethiopic Martyrdoms, pt. 1).

GERMAN AND COPTIC

Schmidt, Carl, ed. *Acta Pauli aus der Heidelberger koptischen Papyrushandschrift Nr. 1*. Leipzig: J. C. Hinrichs, 1904. Text in German and Coptic, discussion in German. Reprint, Hildesheim: G. Olms, 1965.

———. *Acta Pauli Tafelband aus der Heidelberger koptischen Papyrushandschrift Nr. 1*. Leipzig: J. C. Hinrichs, 1904 (Veröffentlichungen aus der Heidelberger Papyrus-Sammlung 2). Reprint: Hildesheim: G. Olms, 1965.

GERMAN AND GREEK

Schmidt, Carl, and Wilhelm Schubart, eds. *Praexeis Paulou Acta Pauli nach dem Papyrus der Hamburger Staats- und Universitäts-Bibliothek.* Glückstadt and Hamburg: J. J. Augustin, 1936.

GREEK AND FRENCH

Vouaux, Leon, trans. *Les Actes de Paul et ses lettres apocryphes: Introduction, textes, traduction et commentaire.* Paris: Letouzey et Ané, 1913 (Les Apocryphes du Nouveau Testament). Text in Greek and French, commentary in French.

LATIN

Gebhardt, Oskar Leopold von, ed. *Passio S. Theclae virginis; die lateinischen Übersetzungen der Acta Pauli et Theclae nebst Fragmenten.* Leipzig: J. C. Hinrichs, 1902 (Texte und Untersuchungen zur Geschichte der altchristlichen Literatur 22/2; n.s., 7/2). Text in Latin, critical apparatus in German, Latin, Greek, and English.

SWEDISH

Carlé, Birte. *Thekla: En kvindeskikkelse i tidlig kristen fortallekunst.* Copenhagen: Delta, 1980. "Fortallingen om Thekla," pp. 9–25.

Acts of John

ENGLISH

See: Hennecke, Schneemelcher, Elliot, and James, above.

SELECTIONS (ENGLISH)

"Acts of John." In Elizabeth A. Clark, trans., *Women in the Early Church,* pp. 88–96.

GREEK AND FRENCH

Festugière, A. J. *Les Actes apocryphes de Jean et de Thomas.* Geneva: P. Cramer, 1983 (Cahiers d'orientalisme 6).

Junod, Eric, and Jean-Daniel Kaestli, eds. *Acta Iohannis.* 2 vols. Turnhout: Brepols, 1983 (Corpus christianorum series apocryphorum 1–2). Greek text and French translation on opposite pages.

GREEK

Zahn, Theodor, ed. *Acta Joannis.* Erlangen: A. Deichert, 1880. Introduction in German, text chiefly in Greek, with some passages in German or Latin. Reprint, Hildesheim: Gerstenberg, 1975.

ITALIAN AND GREEK

Corsaro, Francesco, ed. *Le Praxeis di Giovanni.* Catania: Centro di Studi sull'Antico Cristianesimo, Università di Catania, 1968 (Miscellanea di studi di letteratura cristiana antica 18). Text in Greek, with Italian translation. Bibliography, pp. 203–5.

Gnostic Texts

In 1945 a group of manuscripts was discovered near Chenoboskion in southern Egypt. This library consisted of thirteen codices (books), each containing several works. In addition, a papyrus manuscript (BG 8502) that had been published in the late nineteenth century was recognized as being closely related to these documents. The fifty-two works demonstrate considerable variety in content, but as a whole the library seems to have served a gnostic Christian community. Gnosticism was a form of philosophy and religion that generally opposed spirit to matter. The term *gnostic* derives from the Greek word for knowledge — the revelation of arcane knowledge from the realms of the spirit is frequently the means of enlightenment for the gnostic. The presence of various forms of feminine imagery and other ways in which the interests of women are served in the Nag Hammadi texts have led a number of scholars to believe that some of these anonymous texts were written by women. The four most frequently named candidates are listed below.

Hypostasis of the Archons

Bullard, Roger A., and Bentley Layton, trans. "The Hypostasis of the Archons (II, 4)." In James Robinson, ed., *The Nag Hammadi Library in English,* pp. 161–69.

Layton, Bentley, trans. "The Reality of the Rulers." In Layton, trans., *The Gnostic Scriptures,* pp. 65–76.

On the Origin of the World

Bethge, Hans-Gebhard, et al., trans. "On the Origin of the World (II 97, 24–127, 17)." In James Robinson, ed., *The Nag Hammadi Library in English,* pp. 170–89.

The Thunder, Perfect Mind

MacRae, George W., and Douglas M. Parrot, trans. "The Thunder, Perfect Mind (VI, 2)." In James Robinson, ed., *The Nag Hammadi Library in English,* pp. 295–303.

Layton, Bentley, trans. "The Thunder — Perfect Intellect." In Layton, trans., *The Gnostic Scriptures,* pp. 77–85.

The Gospel of Mary

King, Karen L., et al., trans. "The Gospel of Mary (BG8502, 1)." In James Robinson, ed., *The Nag Hammadi Library in English,* pp. 523–27.

ENGLISH

Robinson, James, ed. *The Nag Hammadi Library in English.* 3d ed., completely revised. San Francisco: Harper and Row, 1988.

Layton, Bentley, trans. *The Gnostic Scriptures: A New Translation with Annotations and Introductions.* Garden City, N.Y.: Doubleday, 1987.

SELECTIONS

Bethge, Hans-Gebhard, et al., trans. "On the Origin of the World (II 97, 24–127, 17)." In Serinity Young, ed., *An Anthology of Sacred Texts by and about Women,* pp. 53–55.

Isenberg, W. W., trans. "The Gospel of Mary." In Amy G. Oden, ed., *In Her Words: Women's Writings in the History of Christian Thought,* pp. 17–25.

King, Karen L., et al., trans. "The Gospel of Mary (BG 7, 1–19, 5)." In Serinity Young, ed., *An Anthology of Sacred Texts by and about Women,* pp. 56–57.

CRITICAL EDITION (COPTIC, ARABIC, AND ENGLISH)

Facsimile Edition of the Nag Hammadi Codices. Leiden: E. J. Brill, 1972–84.

CRITICAL EDITION (COPTIC AND ENGLISH)

Layton, Bentley, ed. *Nag Hammadi Codex II, 2–7: Together with XIII, 2, Brit. Lib. Or. 4926(1), and P.OXY. 1, 654, 655: With Contributions by Many Scholars.* Leiden: Brill, 1989 (Nag Hammadi Studies 20–21; The Coptic Gnostic Library).

Parrot, Douglas M., ed. *Nag Hammadi Codices V, 2–5 and VI; with Papyrus Berolinensis 8502, 1 and 4.* Leiden: Brill, 1979 (Nag Hammadi Studies 11; Coptic Gnostic Library).

COPTIC AND FRENCH

Barc, Bernard, trans. *L'hypostase des archontes: Traité gnostique sur l'origine de l'homme, du monde et des archontes (NH II, 4).* Quebec: Presses de l'Université Laval, 1980 (Bibliothèque copte de Nag Hammadi; sec. "Textes" 5).

Pasquier, Anne, trans. *L'évangile selon Marie (BG 1).* Quebec: Presses de l'Université Laval, 1983 (Bibliothèque copte de Nag Hammadi; sec. "Textes" 10).

Pistis Sophia (third or fourth century)

Pistis Sophia is a long work in Coptic that exists in a manuscript that came to light in England in the eighteenth century. In it, Jesus speaks with several people, notably Mary Magdalene, who is called Mariam or Maria in the text. She asks questions and gives interpretations of Jesus' words. It is possible that underlying these are the words of a woman or women; see book 1, chapters 17–27, 60–62; book 3, chapters 112–35.

COPTIC AND ENGLISH

Schmidt, Carl, ed., and Violet McDermot, trans. *Pistis Sophia.* Leiden: Brill, 1978 (Nag Hammadi Studies 9; Coptic Gnostic Library).

CRITICAL EDITION

Schmidt, Carl, ed. *Koptisch-gnostische Schriften, Bd. 1: Pistis Sophia. Die Beiden Bücher des Jeu. Unbekanntes altgnostisches Werk.* Leipzig, 1905 (Die griechischen christlichen Schriftsteller der ersten drei Jahrhunderte 13); later editions: Berlin: Akademie Verlag, 1954, 1959 (ed. W. Till).

Montanist Oracles

Montanus was a Christian from Phrygia (modern western Turkey). Shortly after the middle of the second century he began to prophesy that an outpouring of the Holy Spirit and the descent of the heavenly Jerusalem would occur very soon. Montanism was particularly strong in Roman Africa where the theologian Tertullian became an adherent in his later days. This has led some to observe that Perpetua may have been influenced by Montanism. Women played a prominent role in the sect that came to be called Montanism by its orthodox opponents. There were a number of female prophets, and Maximilla is reputed to have been the leader of Montanism after the death of Montanus. No writings from the Montanists survive, but a few oracles and other statements have been preserved in quotations by other authors, usually their opponents. These scattered references have been gathered in the publication (Heine) cited below.

Maximilla

See Heine, pp. 2–5.

Priscilla/Prisca

See Heine, pp. 4–5.

Quintilla or Priscilla

See Heine, pp. 4–5.

Unidentified

See Heine, pp. 6–7.

GREEK AND ENGLISH

Heine, Ronald E., ed. *The Montanist Oracles and Testimonia.* Macon, Ga.: Mercer University Press; Louvain: Peeters, 1989 (North American Patristic Society/Patristic Monograph Series 14).

Huber, Elaine C. *Women and the Authority of Inspiration: A Reexamination of Two Prophetic Movements from a Contemporary Feminist Perspective.* Lanham, Md.: University Press of America, 1985. Text and translation of Oracles, pp. 218–22.

Perpetua (d. 203)

Perpetua was about twenty years old, the mother of a small child, and a catechumen preparing to be baptized in the Christian church when she was arrested in her home city of Carthage for not offering the prescribed sacrifice to the Roman gods. The core of the document that survives to tell her story is a poignant first person account of Perpetua's imprisonment and of several visions she had during this time. Perpetua came from the upper social classes and demonstrates her ability to assert herself on her own behalf and on behalf of the other Christians imprisoned with her. While someone else wrote the introduction and the concluding account of her death, most scholars accept that Perpetua wrote or dictated the first person passages. Perpetua was recognized as a saint by orthodox writers from very early on, but some scholars connect her with the Montanist movement because of the views she expresses.

FOR DISCUSSION OF PERPETUA'S AUTHORSHIP:

Dronke, Peter. *Women Writers of the Middle Ages,* pp. 1–17.

ENGLISH AND LATIN

Musurillo, Herbert, ed. and trans. *The Acts of the Christian Martyrs.* Oxford: Clarendon, 1972 (Oxford Early Christian Texts). Parallel Greek or Latin texts with English translations, pp. 106–31.

ENGLISH

Shewring, W. H., trans. *The Passion of SS. Perpetua and Felicity...with the Sermons of S. Augustine upon These Saints...* London: Sheed and Ward, 1931.

Muncey, Raymond Waterville Luke, trans. *The Passion of S. Perpetua.* London: J. M. Dent, 1927.

Owen, Edward Charles Everard, ed. and trans. *Some Authentic Acts of the Early Martyrs.* Oxford: Clarendon, 1927.

TRANSLATIONS IN ANTHOLOGIES

Franz, Marie Louise von, trans. *The Passion of Perpetua.* Irving, Tex.: Spring Publications, 1980 (Jungian Classics Series 3). Slightly revised version of *Passio Perpetua,* which was first published in *Spring* (Irving, Tex.), in 1949. Includes English translation of the text of Perpetua's visions.

"The Martyrdom of Perpetua and Felicitas." In Elizabeth A. Clark, trans., *Women in the Early Church,* pp. 97–106.

Musurillo, H. R., trans. "A Christian Woman's Account of Her Persecution: The Martyrdom of Saints Perpetua and Felicitas." In Ross Shepard Kraemer, ed., *Maenads, Martyrs, Matrons, Monastics,* pp. 96–107.

———. "The Martyrdom of Perpetua." In Barbara J. MacHaffie, ed., *Readings in Her Story,* pp. 24–27.

———. "The Passion of SS. Perpetua and Felicitas." In Elizabeth Petroff, ed., *Medieval Women's Visionary Literature,* pp. 70–77.

"Passion of Perpetua and Felicitas and Their Companions." In Edward R. Hardy, ed., *Faithful Witnesses: Records of Early Christian Martyrs.* London: United Society for Christian Literature and Lutterworth Press, 1960 (World Christian Books, 2d ser. 31) pp. 36–54.

"Prisoner, Dreamer, Martyr: Perpetua of Carthage." In Marcelle Thiébaux, trans., *The Writings of Medieval Women,* 2d ed., pp. 3–21.

Rader, Rosemary, trans. "The Martyrdom of Perpetua." In Serinity Young, ed., *An Anthology of Sacred Texts by and about Women,* p. 46.

———. "The Martyrdom of Perpetua: A Protest Account of Third-century Christianity." In Patricia Wilson-Kastner, ed., *A Lost Tradition: Women Writers of the Early Church*, pp. 1–32.

———. "Perpetua, *The Martyrdom of Perpetua*." In Amy G. Oden, ed., *In Her Words: Women's Writings in the History of Christian Thought*, pp. 26–37.

Wallis, R. E., trans. "The Martyrdom of Perpetua and Felicitas." In *The Ante-nicene Fathers*. Vol. 3: *Latin Christianity: Its founder, Tertullian*. Reprint, Grand Rapids: Eerdmans, 1980, pp. 697–706.

CRITICAL EDITIONS

Beek, Cornelius Johannes Maria Joseph van, ed. *Passio sanctarum Perpetuae et Felicitatis*. Nijmegen: Deker and an de Vegt, 1936.

Robinson, Joseph Armitage, ed. *Passio sanctarum Perpetuae et Felicitatis: The Passion of S. Perpetua, Newly Edited from the MSS. with an Introduction and Notes*. Cambridge: Cambridge University Press, 1891 (Texts and Studies; Contributions to Biblical and Patristic Literature 1/2). Reprint, Nendeln/Liechtenstein: Kraus Reprint Limited, 1967. Latin and Greek on facing pages.

GREEK

Harris, James Rendel, and Seth Kelley Gifford, eds. *The Acts of the Martyrdom of Perpetua and Felicitas: The Original Greek Text Now First Edited from a MS. in the Library of the Convent of the Holy Sepulchre at Jerusalem*. London: C. J. Clay, 1890.

LATIN

Halporn, James W., ed. *Passio sanctarum Perpetuae et Felicitatis*. Bryn Mawr, Pa.: Thomas Library, Bryn Mawr College, 1984 (Bryn Mawr Latin Commentaries). Text in Latin, commentary in English.

LATIN AND GREEK

Beek, Cornelius Johannes Maria Joseph van, ed. *Passio sanctarum Perpetuae et Felicitatis: Latine et Graece*. Bonn: P. Hanstein, 1938 (Florilegium patristicum, fasc. 43). Introduction and notes in Latin. This is the text of a somewhat later variant edition of the work, known as the *Acta minora*.

Franchi de' Cavalieri, Pio Pietro, ed. *La Passio ss. Perpetuae et Felicitatis*. Rome: Herder, 1896.

OTHER LANGUAGES

Habermehl, Peter. *Perpetua und der Ägypter oder Bilder des Bösen im frühen afrikanischen Christentum: Ein Versuch zur Passio sanctarum Perpetuae et Felicitatis.* Berlin: Akademie Verlag, 1992 (Texte und Untersuchungen zur Geschichte der Altchristlichen Literatur 140). Latin text with German translation, pp. 5–29.

Mazzucco, Clementina. *"E fui fatta maschio": La donna nel Cristianesimo primitivo (secoli I–III): Con un'appendice sulla Passio Perpetuae.* Florence: Casa Editrice Le Lettere, 1989 (Letterature/Università degli studi di Torino. Fondo di studi Parini-Chirio 1). Translation on pp. 142–61.

Salonius, Aarne Henrik, trans. *Passio S. Perpetuae Kritische bemerkungen mit besonderer berücksichtigung der griechisch lateinischen überlieferung des textes.* Helsinki: Helsingfors Centraltryckeri Och Bokbinderi Aktiebolag, 1921.

Desert Mothers (fourth and fifth centuries)

The early ascetic monastic movements of hermits in the Egyptian desert included women as well as men. The sayings attributed to a few of them are included among the collections of *Apophthegmata Patrum* or "Sayings of the Fathers."

Sarah (Sarra)

ENGLISH

Ward, Benedicta, trans. *The Desert Christian,* pp. 229–30.
——. *The Sayings of the Desert Fathers,* pp. 171, 192–93.

SELECTIONS

Kraemer, Ross Shepard, ed. *Maenads, Martyrs, Matrons, Monastics,* p. 117.

GREEK AND FRENCH

Guy, Jean-Claude, ed. and trans. *Les apophtegmes des Pères,* 5:13, 14 (pp. 252–53); 7:26 (pp. 356–57).

Syncletica

ENGLISH

Ward, Benedicta, trans. *The Desert Christian,* pp. 230–35.
———. *The Sayings of the Desert Fathers,* pp. 193–97.

SELECTIONS

Kraemer, Ross Shepard, ed. *Maenads, Martyrs, Matrons, Monastics,* pp. 118–22
Wright, J. Robert, ed. *Readings for the Daily Office from the Early Church,* pp. 88–89

GREEK AND FRENCH

Guy, Jean-Claude, ed. and trans. *Les apophtegmes des Pères,* 2:27 (pp. 138–39); 3:34 (pp. 168–69); 4:49–51, 102 (pp. 210–13, 236–37); 6:16, 17 (pp. 324–27); 7:22–25 (pp. 350–57); 8:24, 25 (pp. 416–17).

Theodora

ENGLISH

Ward, Benedicta. *The Desert Christian,* pp. 82–84.
———. *The Sayings of the Desert Fathers,* pp. 71–72.

SELECTIONS

Kraemer, Ross Shepard, ed. *Maenads, Martyrs, Matrons, Monastics,* pp. 123–24.

SOURCES

ENGLISH

Ward, Benedicta. *The Desert Christian: Sayings of the Desert Fathers.* New York: Macmillan, 1980.
———. *The Sayings of the Desert Fathers: The Alphabetical Collection.* London: Mowbray; Kalamazoo, Mich.: Cistercian Publications, 1975.

FRENCH AND GREEK

Guy, Jean-Claude, ed. and trans. *Les apophtegmes des Pères: Collection systématique.* Paris: Cerf, 1993– (Sources chrétiennes 387).

GREEK

Patrologia cursus completus, series graeca. Paris: J. P. Migne, 1868, vol. 65, cols. 71–440.

Epitaphs and Inscriptions by Women
(second to sixth centuries)

Inscriptions on graves and other monuments from the late Roman Empire yield texts from women. These are often from people who would not have otherwise composed texts to be published or preserved.

ENGLISH (QUOTATION AND DISCUSSION)

Dronke, Peter. *Women Writers of the Middle Ages,* pp. 24–26.
Kraemer, Ross Shepard, ed. *Maenads, Martyrs, Matrons, Monastics,* pp. 112–16.

LATIN

Geist, H., and G. Pfohl, eds. *Römische Grabinschriften.* Munich: E. Heimeran, 1976 (Tusculum Bücherei). 1st ed., 1969. Nos. 25, 26, 27, 47, 82, 108, 122, 329, 476, 486, 530. See especially inscription by *HELPIS,* no. 486.
Diehl, E., ed. *Inscriptiones latinae christianae veteres.* 3 vols. Berlin: Weidmann, 1961, nos. 3484, 3885.
Bücheler, Francis, ed. *Carmina latina epigraphica.* 2 vols. Leipzig: Teubner, 1895–97. Supp. 1926. Nos. 66, 369, 537, 1138, 1263, 1979.
Dessau, H., ed. *Inscriptiones latinae selectae.* 3 vols. in 5. Berlin: Weidmann, 1892–1916. Nos. 8142, 8453.
Corpus inscriptorum latinarum. Berlin: Reimarum, 1863– . vol. 2:3596; 12:5193

Macrina (life by her brother Gregory of Nyssa) (c. 327–79)

Macrina was the older sister of Basil the Great and Gregory of Nyssa, the renowned Cappadocian Fathers who were very influential in the development of Christian doctrine. Macrina had an enormous influence over her brothers, convincing Basil to abandon a promising secular career and become a monk. She herself was the head of a religious community that she founded on the family estate. Macrina did not actually write anything that still exists. However, Gregory's *Life of Saint Macrina* recounts several conversations with her, including her visions on her deathbed. This is a first person account by her brother. Scholars believe that it may contain a good deal of Macrina's self-revelation through her relationship and perhaps instructions to her brother. Gregory also featured Macrina as a participant in a philosophical dialogue, *De anima et resurrectione* (On the soul and the resurrection), much as Plato used Socrates. It is difficult to gauge to what extent this text reflects Macrina herself and how much it is simply the tribute of a brother who puts his own best thoughts on the lips of his deceased sister.

Gregory of Nyssa's *Life*

ENGLISH

Callahan, Virginia Woods, trans. Gregory of Nyssa, *Ascetical Works.* Washington: Catholic University of America Press, 1967 (Fathers of the Church 58) pp. 161–91.

Corrigan, Kevin, trans. *The Life of Saint Macrina.* Toronto: Peregrina, 1989, 1987.

Life of St. Macrina. Willits, Calif.: Eastern Orthodox Books, 1974.

Clarke, W. K. Lowther, trans. *The Life of St. Macrina.* London: Society for Promoting Christian Knowledge, 1916 (Early Church Classics).

SELECTIONS

Callahan, Virginia Woods, trans. "Gregory of Nyssa — Life of Macrina." In Serinity Young, ed., *An Anthology of Sacred Texts by and about Women*, p. 57.

———. "The Life of St. Macrina." In Elizabeth Petroff, ed., *Medieval Women's Visionary Literature,* pp. 77–82.

"Life of St. Macrina." In Elizabeth A. Clark, trans., *Women in the Early Church,* pp. 235–43.

Wright, J. Robert, ed. *Readings for the Daily Office from the Early Church,* pp. 217–18.

GREEK

Maraval, Pierre, ed. *Vie de sainte Macrine.* Paris: Cerf, 1971 (Sources chrétiennes 178). Greek text and French.

Patrologia cursus completus, series graeca. Paris: J. P. Migne, 1858, vol. 46, cols. 959–1000. Greek and Latin.

CRITICAL EDITION

Callahan, Virginia Woods, ed. "Vita S. Macrinae." In Werner Wilhelm Jaeger, ed., *Gregorii Nysseni opera: Auxilio aliorum virorum doctorum.* Leiden: Brill, 1952–. vol. 8, pt. 1, pp. 345–416. Text in Greek, introductory matter in Latin.

OTHER LANGUAGES

Giannarelli, Elena, trans. *La vita di S. Macrina.* Milan: Edizioni Paoline, 1988 (Letture cristiane del primo millennio 4).

De anima et resurrectione (On the soul and the resurrection)

ENGLISH

Callahan, Virginia Woods, trans. Gregory of Nyssa, *Ascetical Works.* Washington: Catholic University of America Press, 1967 (Fathers of the Church 58) pp. 195–272.

Roth, Catharine P., trans. *The Soul and the Resurrection.* Crestwood, N.Y.: St. Vladimir's Seminary Press, 1992.

Wilson, H. A., trans. *On the Soul and the Resurrection.* In Henry Wace, ed., *Select Writings and Letters of Gregory, Bishop of Nyssa.* Reprint (1892), Grand Rapids: Eerdmans, 1979 (Nicene and Post-Nicene Fathers, 2d ser. 8) pp. 428–68.

SELECTIONS

Schaff, Philip, and Henry Wace, trans. "Macrina, *On the Soul and the Resurrection.*" In Amy G. Oden, ed., *In Her Words: Women's Writings in the History of Christian Thought,* pp. 47–66.

GREEK

"De anima et resurrectione dialogus [Peri psyche kai anastaseos ho logos]." In *Patrologia cursus completus, series graeca.* Paris: J. P. Migne, 1858. vol. 46, cols. 11–160.

Proba (fourth century)

A matron of the privileged class in fourth-century Rome, Proba wrote a substantial cento, which used lines from Virgil to tell the Christian story of salvation. This text was relatively popular for study in the Middle Ages, and there are printed versions from as early as the fifteenth century.

ENGLISH AND LATIN

Clark, Elizabeth A., and Diane F. Hatch. *The Golden Bough, the Oaken Cross: The Virgilian Cento of Faltonia Betitia Proba.* Chico, Calif.: Scholars Press, 1981.

SELECTIONS

"Cento." In Elizabeth A. Clark, trans., *Women in the Early Church,* pp. 165–68.

Kastner, G. R., A. Millin, and J. Reedy, trans. "Proba's Cento." In Patricia Wilson-Kastner, ed., *A Lost Tradition: Women Writers of the Early Church,* pp. 33–69.

"Proba." In Helene Homeyer, trans., *Dichterinnen des Altertums und des frühen Mittelalters,* pp. 178–83. German and Latin.

ITALIAN

Cacciari, Antonio, ed. *Epistolae la preghiera: epistola 130 a Proba: Introduzione, traduzione e note.* Rome: Edizioni Paoline, 1981 (Letture cristiane delle origini Testi 11). Italian and Latin.

LATIN

Schenkl, Carolus, ed. "Probae Cento." In Michael Petschenig, ed., *Poetae christiani minores*. Prague and Vienna: F. Tempsky, 1888 (Corpus scriptorum ecclesiasticorum latinorum 16) pp. 511–640. Reprint, New York: Johnson, 1972–.

Patrologia cursus completus, series latina. Paris: J. P. Migne, 1844–66, vol. 19, cols. 801–18.

Egeria (late fourth century)

Egeria made a pilgrimage to the Holy Land in the late fourth century. She was a consecrated virgin (probably a nun), and her work was probably written for the edification of her sisters back home in Spain or southern France. Her account of her pilgrimage is an extremely detailed chronicle of the holy places she visited. This work is especially valuable to liturgical scholars because of her detailed descriptions of the liturgies in Jerusalem during her visit. There has been much confusion over the identity and name of the author of the work, so that older works contain many variations of the names Etheria, Egeria, and Silvia of Aquitaine.

BIBLIOGRAPHY OF WRITINGS CONCERNING EGERIA

Starowieyeski, Marek. "Bibliografia Egeriana." *Augustinianum* 19 (1979) pp. 297–318.

ENGLISH

Hunt, E. D. *Holy Land Pilgrimage in the Later Roman Empire, AD 312–460*. Oxford: Clarendon, 1982.

Wilkinson, John Donald, trans. *Egeria's Travels to the Holy Land: Newly Translated with Supporting Documents and Notes*. Rev. ed. Jerusalem: Ariel; Warminster, Eng.: Aris and Phillips, 1981. 1st ed.: London: SPCK, 1971.

Gingras, George E., trans. *Egeria: Diary of a Pilgrimage*. New York: Newman, 1970 (Ancient Christian Writers: The Works of the Fathers in Translation 38).

McClure, M. L., and C. L. Feltoe, trans. *The Pilgrimage of Etheria.* London: Macmillan, 1919 (Translations of Christian Literature, ser. 3: Liturgical Texts).

Bernard, J. H., trans. *The Pilgrimage of S. Silvia of Aquitania to the Holy Places Circa 385 A.D.* London: Palestine Pilgrim's Text Society, 1891.

SELECTIONS

"The Pilgrimage of Egeria." In Elizabeth A. Clark, trans., *Women in the Early Church,* pp. 186–97.

"A Pilgrim to the Holy Land: Egeria of Spain." In Marcelle Thiébaux, trans., *The Writings of Medieval Women,* pp. 1–14; 2d ed., pp. 23–48.

Wilson-Kastner, Patricia, trans. "Egeria — Account of Her Pilgrimage." In Serinity Young, ed., *An Anthology of Sacred Texts by and about Women,* pp. 51–52.

———. "Egeria, *Pilgrimage (404–417)*." In Amy G. Oden, ed., *In Her Words: Women's Writings in the History of Christian Thought,* pp. 74–83.

———. "Egeria in the Holy Land." In Barbara J. MacHaffie, ed., *Readings in Her Story,* pp. 40–43.

———. "The Pilgrimage of Egeria." In Patricia Wilson-Kastner, ed., *A Lost Tradition: Women Writers of the Early Church,* pp. 71–133.

Wright, J. Robert, ed. *Readings for the Daily Office from the Early Church,* pp. 128, 133, 165, 172, 230, 449, 465.

CRITICAL EDITION

Franceschini, E., and R. Weber. *Itineraria et alia geographica.* Turnhout: Brepols, 1965 (Corpus christianorum series latina 175) pp. 27–103.

CRITICAL EDITION (LATIN AND SPANISH)

Arce, Agustín. *Itinerario de la Virgen Egeria (381–384).* Madrid: Editorial Católica, 1980 (Biblioteca de autores cristianos 416).

LATIN AND FRENCH

Maraval, Pierre, and Manuel C. Díaz y Díaz. *Journal de voyage (itineraire).* Paris: Cerf, 1982 (Sources chrétiennes 296).

Pétré, Hélène. *Journal de Voyage.* Paris: Cerf, 1948 (Sources chrétiennes 21).

LATIN

Prinz, Otto, ed. *Itinerarium Egeriae (Peregrinatio Aetheriae)*. 5th ed. Heidelberg: C. Winter, 1960. Latin text with commentary in German. 1st through 4th eds. published as: Wilhelm Heraeus, ed., *Silviae vel potius Aetheriae Peregrinatio ad loca sancta*. Heidelberg: C. Winter, 1908 (Sammlung vulgärlateinischer Texte 1).

Hamman, A., ed. *Itinerarium Egeriae*. Paris, 1958 (Patrologiae latinae supplementum 1).

Bechtel, S., ed. *Silviae Peregrinatio: Text and a Study of the Latinity*. Chicago, 1902 (Studies in Classical Philology 4).

Geyer, Paul, ed. *Itinera hierosolymitana saecvli IIII–VII*. Vienna and Prague: F. Tempsky; Leipzig: G. Freytag, 1898 (Corpus scriptorum ecclesiasticorum latinorum 39). Reprint: New York: Johnson, 1964.

GERMAN

Donner, Herbert, ed. *Pilgerfahrt ins Heilige Land: Die ältesten Berichte christlicher Palästinapilger (4–7. Jahrhundert)*. Stuttgart: Verlag Katholisches Bibelwerk, 1979, pp. 69–137.

Vretska, K. *Die Pilgerreise der Aetheriae*. Klosterneuberg, 1958. Introduction and commentary by Hélène Pétré.

ITALIAN

Giannarelli, Elena, ed. *Diario di viaggio*. Milan: Edizioni Paoline, 1992 (Letture cristiane del primo millennio; testi 13).

Siniscalco, Paolo, and Lella Scarampi, eds. *Pellegrinaggio in terra santa*. Rome: Città nuova editrice, 1985 (Collana di testi patristici 48).

LATIN AND ITALIAN

Natalucci, Nicoletta, ed. *Pellegrinaggio in Terra Santa = Itinerarium Egeriae*. Firenze: Nardini, 1991 (Biblioteca patristica 17).

Chapter 2 _____

Early Medieval Writings by Women

Poets of Late Antiquity
and the Early Middle Ages

Christian women, especially those of the upper classes, wrote secular poetry in the later Roman Empire and the early Middle Ages.

Pervigilium Veneris

This anonymous poem may have been written by a woman, although a number of male authors have also been suggested. See Laurence Catlow's commentary (cited below) for a full discussion.

LATIN AND ENGLISH

Mackail, John W., ed. and trans. *Catullus, Tibullus and Pervigilium Veneris*. London: Heinemann; New York: Putnam, 1925; Cambridge, Mass.: Harvard University Press, 1962 (Loeb Classical Library 6).

LATIN

Catlow, Laurence. *Pervigilium Veneris*. Brussels: Latomus, 1980 (Collection latomus 172).

LATIN AND FRENCH

Raynaud, Ernest, trans. *Poetae minores: Sabinus, . . . Eucheria, Pervigilium Veneris*. Paris: Garnier, 1931.

Cabaret-Dupaty, M., trans. *Poetae minores: Sabinus, Calpurnius,...
Eucheria, Pervigilium Veneris: Traduction nouvelle.* Paris: C. Panck-
oucke, 1842 (Bibliothèque latine-française depuis Adrien jusqu'à
Grégoire de Tours; 2d ser.).

Sulpicia (fifth century?)

A Latin satire is sometimes attributed to a woman named Sulpicia.
There is, however, much disagreement about both authorship and
date.

FOR DISCUSSION OF AUTHORSHIP

Fuchs, H. "Das Klagelied der Sulpicia." In Marc Sieber, ed., *Discordia
concors: Festgabe für Edgar Bonjour.* Basel and Stuttgart: Helbing
and Lichtenhahn, 1968, 1:32ff.

LATIN AND ITALIAN

Giordano Rampioni, Anna, ed. and trans. *Sulpiciae conquestio (Ep.
Bob. 37).* Bologna: Pàtron Editore, 1982.

LATIN

"Musa, quibus numeris heroas et arma frequentas." In *Epigrammata
Bobiensia,* no. 37 (see next two entries).
Speyer, Wolfgang, ed. *Epigrammata Bobiensia.* Leipzig: Teubner, 1963
(Bibliotheca scriptorum graecorum et romanorum teubnerianas).
Munari, Franco, ed. *Epigrammata Bobiensia.* Rome: Edizioni di Storia
e Letteratura, 1955 (Storia e letteratura 59).

Eudocia (Athenaïs-Eudociae) (400–460)

Eudocia is the Christian name of the wife of Theodosius II. Before her baptism and marriage, her name was Athenaïs. Eudocia
(also spelled Eudokia) was well known for her poetry. Some of
her letters to popes and emperors also survive.

Letter to Theodosius II

Schwartz, Eduard, ed. *Acta conciliorum oecumenorum.* Berlin and Leipzig: De Gruyter, 1935, tome 2, vol. 3, pt. 1; *Epistularum ante Gesta Collectio,* no. 21 (p. 15).

Patrologia cursus completus, series latina. Paris: J. P. Migne, 1844–66, vol. 54, cols. 905–8.

Martyrdom of Saint Cyprian

ENGLISH (SELECTIONS)

"Calumniated Empress and Poet: Eudocia of Constantinople." In Marcelle Thiébaux, trans., *The Writings of Medieval Women,* 2d ed., pp. 49–69.

Kastner, G. R., trans. "The Martyrdom of St. Cyprian." In Patricia Wilson-Kastner, ed., *A Lost Tradition: Women Writers of the Early Church,* pp. 135–71.

GERMAN AND LATIN (SELECTIONS)

Homeyer, Helene, trans. *Dichterinnen des altertums und des frühen Mittelalters.* Paderborn: Schöningh, 1979, pp. 113–33.

LATIN

Ludwich, Arthur, ed. *Eudociae Augustae, Procli Lycii, Claudiani carminum graecorum reliquiae.* Leipzig: Teubner, 1897 (Bibliotheca scriptorum graecorum et romanorum teubneriana).

Ludwich, Arthur, ed. *Eudociae Augustae carminum reliquiae.* Königsburg: Hartungiana, 1893.

Gregorovius, Ferdinand Adolf, ed. *Athenaïs: Geschichte einer byzantinischen kaiserin.* 2d ed. Leipzig: F. A. Brockhaus, 1882. "Cyprianus und Justina, dichtung der kaiserin Eudokia. 2. gesang: Das bekenntniss des Cyprianus," pp. [265]–87.

Patrologia cursus completus, series graeca. Paris: J. P. Migne, 1844–66, vol. 85.

Other Works

Dios, Wolfgang, ed. *The Byzantine Plays: Boethius and Athenaïs.* Toronto: Wayfare, 1991.

Green, Judith, and Yoram Tsafrir, eds. "Greek Inscriptions from Hammat Gader: A Poem by the Empress Eudocia and Two Building Inscriptions." *Israel Exploration Journal* 32 (1982) pp. 77–96.

Gregorovius, Ferdinand, and Fritz Schillmann, eds. *Athen und Athenaïs, Schicksale einer Stadt und einer Kaiserin im Byzantinischen Mittelalter.* Dresden: W. Jess, 1927.

Sattler, Gustav, ed. *De Eudociae Homerocentonibus.* Bayreuth: L. Ellwanger, 1904. In Greek or Latin. Programm. — K.b. humanistisches Gymnasium, Bayreuth, 1903/1904.

Eucheria (sixth century)

Eucheria was a prosperous woman from Marseilles, known only from a few poems. She was part of the circle that included Venantius Fortunatus and Radegunde, although her poetry appears more secular in its interest.

ENGLISH

"From a Literary Circle in Provence: Eucheria of Marseilles." In Marcelle Thiébaux, trans., *The Writings of Medieval Women,* pp. 63–64.

"Words Flowing Like Gold Fringes: An Anonymous Letter Writer of the Sixth Century; Eucheria of Marseilles." In Marcelle Thiébaux, trans., *The Writings of Medieval Women,* 2d ed., pp. 125–34.

GERMAN/LATIN

Homeyer, Helene, trans. *Dichterinnen des Altertums und des frühen Mittelalters.* Paderborn: Schöningh, 1979, pp. 185–87.

LATIN

Baehrens, Emil, ed. *Poetae Latinae minores.* Leipzig: Teubner, 1883 (Bibliotheca scriptorum graecorum et romanorum teubneriana). Reprint: New York: Garland, 1979, vol. 5, p. 361.

Buecheler, Francis, and Alexander Riese, eds. *Anthologia latina.* Leipzig: Teubner, 1894 (Bibliotheca scriptorum graecorum et romanorum teubneriana) vol. 1, fasc. i, no. 390.

Cabaret-Dupaty, M. *Poetae minores.* Paris: C. Panckoucke, 1842 (Bibliothèque latine-française depuis Adrien jusqu'à Grégoire de Tours, 2d ser.) pp. 408–16.

Extant Correspondence of Ancient Women

The exchange of letters was quite common in antiquity, and literate women certainly wrote and received letters in proportion to their means, social standing, and the importance of the business they needed to transact by letter. People of less education, even those who could read and write in a very basic fashion, normally had important business correspondence drafted for them by notaries, a fact that should be kept in mind when interpreting ancient letters. Only the letters of people who were considered very important would have been preserved over a thousand years, and then only those that were considered most interesting. Thus only a few letters by women survive, and these have usually been found among the correspondence of popes, emperors, and great theologians.

CIRCLE OF SAINT JEROME (before 419)

Saint Jerome maintained correspondence with various women. Only one letter written by women survives: from Jerome's friends Paula and Eustochium encouraging their friend Marcella to visit the Holy Land. This letter was often attributed to Jerome in the past, but the arguments hinged on women not being able to write such a letter.

FOR DISCUSSION OF JEROME'S FEMALE CORRESPONDENTS AND
THE AUTHORSHIP OF THE LETTER

Dronke, Peter. *Women Writers of the Middle Ages,* pp. 17–19.
Clark, Elizabeth A. *Jerome, Chrysostom and Friends: Essays and Translations.* New York and Toronto: Edwin Mellen Press, 1979 (Studies in Women and Religion 1).

Paula and Eustochium

Letter to Marcella

ENGLISH

Dronke, Peter. *Women Writers of the Middle Ages,* pp. 17–19. Excerpts.

LATIN

Ruíz Bueno, Daniel, ed. *Cartas de San Jerónomo.* Madrid: Editorial
Católica, 1962. 2 vols. (Biblioteca de autores cristianos 219–29;
sec. 3: Santos Padres) 1:318–34.

Hilberg, Isodorus. *Sancti Eusebii hieronymi epistulae.* Pt. 1. Vienna:
F. Tempsky; Leipzig: G. Freytag, 1905 (Corpus scriptorum ecclesiasticorum latinorum 54) Ep. 46, pp. 329–44.

CIRCLE OF EMPEROR THEODOSIUS II (fifth century)

Eudocia (Athenaïs-Eudociae). *See above* pp. 52–54

Galla Placida

Letters to Theodosius II and Pulcheria

Schwartz, Eduard, ed. *Acta conciliorum oecumenorum.* Berlin and Leipzig: De Gruyter, 1935. Tome 2, vol. 3, pt. 1: *Epistularum ante gesta
collectio,* nos. 18 and 20 (pp. 13–14).

Patrologia cursus completus, series latina. Paris: J. P. Migne, 1844–66.
vol. 54, cols. 859–62, 863–67.

Pulcheria

Letter to Pope Leo I

Schwartz, Eduard, ed. *Acta conciliorum oecumenorum.* Berlin and Leipzig: De Gruyter, 1935. Tome 2, vol. 3, pt. 1: *Epistularum ante gesta
collectio,* no. 29 (pp. 18–19).

Patrologia cursus completus, series latina. Paris: J. P. Migne, 1844–66,
vol. 54, cols. 905–8.

CORRESPONDENTS OF POPE HORMISDAS (Pope 514–23)

Anastasia

Guenther, Otto. *Epistulae imperatorum Pontificium Aliorum... Avellana Quae Dicitur Collectio.* Vienna and Prague: F. Tempsky; Leipzig: G. Freytag, 1895–98 (Corpus scriptorum ecclesiasticorum latinorum 35, pt. 2) Ep. 165, p. 616

Patrologia cursus completus, series latina. Paris: J. P. Migne, 1844–66. v. 63, col. 451–52.

Euphemia

Guenther, Otto, ed. *Epistulae imperatorum Pontificium Aliorum... Avellana Quae Dicitur Collectio.* Vienna and Prague: F. Tempsky; Leipzig: G. Freytag, 1895–98 (Corpus scriptorum ecclesiasticorum latinorum 35, pt. 2) Ep. 194, p. 652.)

Juliana Anicia

Guenther, Otto, ed. *Epistulae imperatorum Pontificium Aliorum... Avellana Quae Dicitur Collectio.* Vienna and Prague: F. Tempsky; Leipzig: G. Freytag, 1895–98 (Corpus scriptorum ecclesiasticorum latinorum 35, pt. 2) Ep. 164, pp. 615, 657–58.

Patrologia cursus completus, series latina. Paris: J. P. Migne, 1844–66. v. 63 col. 451.

OTHER LETTERS

Brunhilda (late sixth century)

Brunhilda was queen of the Visigothic kingdom of Austrasia. These letters are chiefly her correspondence with Empress Anastasia of Constantinople in which Brunhilda seeks the release of her daughter and infant grandson, who had been captured by the Greeks.

Letters (nos. 26, 27, 29, 30, 44) in W. Gundlach, ed., *Epistulae austrasicae.* In Henri Rochais, ed., *Liber scintillarum.* Turnhout: Brepols, 1957 (Corpus christianorum, series latina 117) pp. 450–67.

Herchenafreda (beginning of the seventh century)

The life of Saint Desiderius contains several letters from his mother, Herchenafreda, in which she sought to persuade him to accept the position of bishop of Cahors, which was left vacant by the murder of his brother Rusticus.

Letters to her son Desiderius in B. Krusch, ed., *Vita S. Desiderii*. In Henri Rochais, ed., *Liber scintillarum*. Turnhout: Brepols, 1957 (Corpus christianorum, series latina 117) pp. 353–56.

Amalaswintha (c. 494–535)

SELECTIONS (ENGLISH)

"An Ill-fated Gothic Queen: Amalasuntha of Italy." In Marcelle Thié-baux, trans., *The Writings of Medieval Women*, pp. 15–23; 2d ed., pp. 71–84.

LATIN

Mommsen, Theodor, and Ludwig Traube, eds. *Cassiodori Senatoris Variae* (Monumenta germaniae historica: Auctorum antiquissimo-rum 12) bk. 10, pp. 296, 298–99, 303, 304.

Gudelina (sixth century)

Two letters in Cassiodorus, *Variae* 10.21, 24

Mommsen, Theodor and Ludwig Traube, eds. *Cassiodori Senatoris Variae* (Monumentae germaniae historica: Auctorum antiquissino-rum 12) pp. 311, 313.

SOURCES FOR CASSIODORUS'S *VARIAE*

The *Variae* contain the official correspondence of Cassiodorus, for the most part in the name of Theodoric and other Ostrogothic rulers.

ENGLISH

Barnish, S. J. B. *The Variae of Magnus Aurelius Cassiodorus Senator...:*
Being Documents of the Kingdom of the Ostrogoths in Italy.
Liverpool: Liverpool University Press, 1992.

Hodgkin, Thomas, trans. *The Letters of Cassiodorus: Being a Con-*
densed Translation of the Variae Epistolae of Magnus Aurelius
Cassiodorus Senator. London: H. Frowde, 1886.

CRITICAL EDITIONS (LATIN)

Fridh, Åke J., ed. *Magni Aurelii Cassiodori Senatoris opera.* Turnhout:
Brepols, 1958 (Corpus christianorum, series latina 96–98). Vol. 96
(pt. 1) contains the *Variarum* and was published in 1973.

Mommsen, Theodor, and Ludwig Traube, eds. *Cassiodori Senatoris*
Variae. Berlin: Weidmann, 1894 (Monumenta germaniae historica:
Auctorum antiquissimorum 12).

Burginda (seventh or eighth century)

Sims-Williams, Patrick, ed. "Letter to a Young Man." *Medium Aevum*
48 (1979) pp. 1–22.

Boulogne manuscript 74 carries the name of Burginda. This contains an abridgement of Apponius's commentary on the Song of
Songs.

De Vregille, B., and L. Neyrand, eds. "Expositionis Apponii Sancti Abbatis in Canticum Canticorum Libri XII Breviter Deceptimque." In
Apponii in Canticum canticorum expositionem. Turnhout: Brepols,
1986 (Corpus christianorum, series latina 19).

Radegundis (Saint Radegund) (518–87)
and Her Circle

Radegunde was a Thuringian princess who married a Frankish
king, Clothaire I, after being captured by the Franks. She left him
after his murder of her brother, was ordained a deaconess, and
founded a monastery of nuns outside Poitiers. She was a friend
and correspondent of Venantius Fortunatus, the famous hymn

writer. Her own writings (letters and hymns) have not been preserved except as they may be detected in the writings of Venantius Fortunatus, who collaborated with her on some poetic writings. There are, however, writings by women who knew her and looked to her for advice: Baudonivia (her biographer), Caesaria, and the anonymous correspondent noted below.

ENGLISH

Schwartz, Judy Ann. "The Poems of Venantius Fortunatus to Radegunde and Agnes." Master's thesis, Cornell University, June 1969.

LATIN

Bulst, W. "Radegundis an Amalafred." In *Bibliotheca Docet: Festschrift an Carl Wehmer.* Amsterdam, 1963, pp. 369–80.

Krusch, Bruno, ed. *Venanti Honori Clementiani Fortunati presbyteri italici opera pedestria.* Berlin: Weidmann, 1885 (Monumenta germaniae historica: Auctorum antiquissimorum 4, pars posterior [parts at the end]); *Vita S. Radegundis,* pp. 38–49.

"De excidio Thoringiae" (appendix 1, pp. 271–75); "Ad Artachin" (appendix 3, pp. 278–79). In Fridericus Leo, ed., *Venanti Fortunati opera poetica.* Berlin: Weidmann, 1881 (Monumenta germaniae historica: Auctorum antiquissimorum 4/1).

Patrologia cursus completus, series latina. Paris: J. P. Migne, 1844–66, v. 72.

"Testamentum." In *Diplomata regum Francorum e stirpe Merowingica.* Hannover: Hahn, 1872 (Monumenta germaniae historica, Diplomata 1) pp. 8–11.

ITALIAN

Palermo, Giovanni, ed. Venantius Honorius Clementianus Fortunatus, *Vite dei santi Ilario e Radegonda di Poitiers.* Rome: Città Nuova, 1989 (Collana di testi patristici 81).

Baudonivia (early seventh century)

McCarthy, M. *The Rule for Nuns.* Washington, 1933.

"De vita sanctae Radegundis libri duo." In Bruno Krusch, ed., *Fredegarii et aliorum Chronica: Vitae sanctorum.* Hannover: Hahn,

1888 (Monumenta germaniae historica: Scriptores rerum merovingi-carum 2). Bk. 1 is probably by Venantius Fortunatus; bk. 2 (pp. 377–95) is by Baudonivia.

Caesaria (sixth century)

SELECTIONS

"Early Convent Life: Three Women of Merovingian Gaul: Radegund of Poitiers; Caesaria of Arles; Baudonivia of Poitiers." In Marcelle Thiébaux, trans., *The Writings of Medieval Women*, pp. 25–57; 2d ed., pp. 85–124.

LATIN

Epistolae merowingici et karolini aevi. Berlin: Weidmann, 1892 (Monumenta germaniae historica: Epistolarum 3/1) pp. 450–53.

Anonymous (sixth century)

ENGLISH

"A Learned Woman Writes a Letter: Anonymous." In Marcelle Thiébaux, trans., *The Writings of Medieval Women*, pp. 57–62.
"Words Flowing Like Gold Fringes: An Anonymous Letter Writer of the Sixth Century; Eucheria of Marseilles." In Marcelle Thiébaux, trans., *The Writings of Medieval Women*, 2d ed., pp. 125–34.

LATIN

Epistolae merowingici et karolini aevi. Berlin: Weidmann, 1892 (Monumenta germaniae historica: Epistolarum 3/1) pp. 716–18.
"Nisi, tanti seminis, silentium emum." In C. P. Caspari, ed., *Briefe, Abhandlungen, und Predigten aus den zwei letzten Jahrhunderten des Kirchlichen Alterthums und dem Anfang des Mittelalters.* Christiana: Mallingsche Buchdruckerei, 1890, pp. 178–82.

Chapter 3 _____

The Byzantine Empire and the East

Byzantine Hagiographers

The lives of saints were very important in early Byzantine monastic communities. Some of this literature emerged from the communities of women. While these lives are normally anonymous in authorship, it is sometimes possible to establish that the author was one or more women.

Biographer of Saint Matrona

FOR A DISCUSSION OF THE LIKELIHOOD THAT THE BIOGRAPHY OF SAINT MATRONA WAS WRITTEN BY A NUN OF HER CONVENT

Topping, Eva Catafygiotu. "St. Matrona and Her Friends: Sisterhood in Byzantium." In *Kathegetria*. Camberly: Porphyrogenitus, 1988, pp. 211–24.

ENGLISH

Bennasser, Khalifa Abubakr. "Gender and Sanctity in Early Byzantine Monasticism: A Study of the Phenomenon of Female Ascetics in Male Monastic Habit with a Translation of the Life of St. Matrona." Ph.D. diss., Rutgers University, 1984, pp. 118–77. Available from University Microfilms International, Ann Arbor, Mich.

GREEK AND LATIN

Simon Metaphrastes. *Opera omnia*, t. 3. In *Patrologiae greco-latine*. Paris: J.-P. Migne, 1864, vol. 116, cols. 919–54.
Delehaye, H., ed. *Acta sanctorum*. November [vol.] III, pp. 813–22.

Sergia (seventh century)

Saint Olympias (361–408) was a woman of the aristocracy who used her wealth and influence to help John Chrysostom. After becoming a widow, she was ordained deaconess and founded a convent near Hagia Sophia in Constantinople. She was banished when she refused to accept Chrysostom's successor as patriarch of Constantinople. Chrysostom's letters from their correspondence survive, but not Olympias's to him. Sergia was the head of the convent Olympias founded and was responsible for having her relics transferred there. In conjunction with this, Sergia wrote an account of the translation of the relics that also tells of Olympias.

ENGLISH

"Life of Olympias." In Elizabeth A. Clark, trans., *Women in the Early Church,* pp. 224–31.

"Narration concerning Olympias." In Elizabeth A. Clark, *Jerome, Chrysostom, and Friends: Essays and Translations.* New York and Toronto: Edwin Mellen Press, 1979, pp. 145–57.

CRITICAL EDITION (GREEK AND FRENCH)

Malingrey, Anne-Marie, ed. Saint John Chrysostom. *Lettres à Olympias.* 2d ed. Paris: Cerf, 1968 (Sources chrétiennes 13bis) pp. 393–449.

Byzantine Hymnographers

Kassiane (ninth century)

A nun from Constantinople, Kassiane was probably from an important family. There exists a tradition that she was among the candidates to be married to Emperor Theophilos. Most of her writings were hymns for liturgical use, although she also wrote some secular poetry (*gnomai,* or wise sayings). Listed below are the writings of Kassiane that are generally considered to be authentic. A number of other hymns have been attributed to her, probably since she was the best-known female Byzantine hymnographer, and her troparion for Holy Wednesday is known as "The

Troparion of Kassiane." For a complete catalog and discussion, see Ilse Rochow, *Studien zu der Person*..... The numbers refer to Rochow's catalog. (See the bibliography that comes after the following list for full data on works cited.)

1. Canon for the Dead   Not in official liturgical books

   Kanon anapausimos eis koimesin

   Tripolitis, pp. 88–105.
   Homeyer, pp. 138–53.
   S. Petrides, pp. 243f.; Krumbacher, pp. 347–56; Tzedakes, 1962, pp. 175–97; L. Petit, *Byzantinische Zeitschrift* 7 (1898) pp. 596f.

2. Tetrodion for Holy Saturday   Orthros (Matins) of
                                                   Holy Saturday
                                                   Triodion 407–8

   Only the Hirmoi (*Irmos:* model or connecting stanzas) are extant.

   Kumati thalasses ton krypsanta palai
   He who once hid the pursuing tyrant

   Tripolitis, pp. 80–87.
   H. J. W. Tillyard, *Byzantinische Zeitschrift* 20 (1911) pp. 420–85; Papadopoulos-Kerameneus 2, pp. 164–73; Tzedakes, 1962, pp. 154–56.

3. Troparion of Kassiane   Orthros (Matins) of Holy Wednesday
                                Triodion Eng. 360

   First Line: *Kyrie he en pollais hamartiais peripesousa gune...*
               Lord, the woman fallen into many sins...

   Cassia. "On Mary Magdalene [No. 231]." In Konstantinos Athanasiou Trypanes, comp., *The Penguin Book of Greek Verse.* Harmondsworth, Eng.: Penguin Books, 1971, p. 435.
   Sakelliou, Liana. "Troparion." In Jane Hirshfield, ed., *Women in Praise of the Sacred*, pp. 53–55.

   Tripolitis, pp. 76–79
   Homeyer, pp. 154–55.
   Tillyard, pp. 428, 461–72; Wellesz, pp. 278, 312–14, 353, 395–97; Tzedakes, 1962, p. 153; Petrides, pp. 239f.

4. Sticheron   Vespers of November 15
   Menaion 3.111   Martyrs: Gurias, Samonas, and Abibos

   First Line: *He Edessa Euphraineta, hoti en to soro...*
           Edessa rejoices that she has been enriched by the
           tomb of...

   Tripolitis, pp. 8–9.
   Tillyard, pp. 424–25, 449–51; Papadopoulos, 1956, p. 93; Tzedakes, 1961, pp. 133, 154; Trempelas, p. 248.

5. Sticheron   Ainoi of Orthros (Lauds) December 13
   Menaion 4.112   Martyrs: Eustrakios, Auxentios, Eugenios,
                                        Mardarios, and Orestes

   First Line: *Ten pentachordon lyran kai pentaphoton luchnian...*
           The five-stringed lute and the five-fold lamp...

   Tripolitis, pp. 14–15.
   Tillyard, *Byzantinische Zeitschrift*, pp. 425f., 452–55; Papadopoulos, 1957, p. 7; Tzedakes, 1961, pp. 177f.; Trempelas p. 247.

6. Sticheron   Ainoi of Orthros (Lauds) December 13
   Menaion 4.113   Martyrs: Eustrakios, Auxentios, Eugenios,
                                        Mardarios, and Orestes

   First Line: *Hyper ten ton Hellenon paideian...*
           Above the teachings of the Greeks...

   Tripolitis, pp. 16–17.
   Tillyard, *Byzantinische Zeitschrift*, pp. 426–27, 456; Papadopoulos, 1957, p. 7; Tzedakes, 1961, p. 178; Trempelas, pp. 247f.

7. Sticheron   Vespers on Christmas
   Menaion 4.219
   English: Festal Menaion, p. 254

   First Line: *Augoustou monarchesantos epi tes ges...*
           When Augustus reigned alone upon the earth...

   Tripolitis, pp. 18–19.
   Homeyer, pp. 152–53.
   Tillyard, *Byzantinische Zeitschrift*, pp. 457–60; Tillyard, *Byzantine Music and Hymnology*, p. 29; Reese, p. 82; Tzedakes, 1961,
   pp. 178, 191.

   See Rochow, p. 224 n. 332 for further bibliography.

22. Sticheron   Vespers of June 24
    Menaion 10.88   Birth of John the Baptist

    First Line: *Esaiou nun tou prophetou he phone*...
         Now the voice of Isaiah the prophet...

    Tripolitis, pp. 50–51.
    Tillyard, *Byzantinische Zeitschrift,* 429f., 476–78; Tzedakes, 1962, p. 32; Trempelas, p. 248.

23. Sticheron   Vespers of June 29
    Menaion 10.113   Saints Peter and Paul

    First line: *Tous phosteras tous megalous tes ekklesias*...
         Let us praise Peter and Paul the great luminaries of...

    Tripolitis, 52–53.
    Tillyard, *Byzantinische Zeitschrift,* pp. 423, 446–48; Tillyard, *Byzantine Music and Hymnody,* pp. 52–54; Papadopoulos, 1956, p. 53; Tzedakes, 1962, p. 48.

FOR A COMPLETE CATALOG OF KASSIANE'S WORKS AND A STUDY OF HER LIFE AND WORKS

Rochow, Ilse. *Studien zu der Person, den Werken und dem Nachleben der Dichterin Kassia.* Berlin: Akademie-Verlag, 1967 (Berliner Byzantinistische Arbeiten 38).

SOURCES

ENGLISH: SCHOLARLY EDITIONS

Tripolitis, Antonia. *Kassia: The Legend, the Woman, and Her Work.* New York: Garland, 1992 (Garland Library of Medieval Literature 84: ser. A). English and Greek. Complete hymns, epigrams, and gnomic verses.

Wellesz, E. *A History of Byzantine Music and Hymnography.* Rev. ed. Oxford: Oxford University Press, 1961.

Reese, Gustave. *Music in the Middle Ages.* New York: Norton, 1940.

Tillyard, Henry J. W. *Byzantine Music and Hymnography.* New York: AMS Press, 1976. Reprint of the 1923 ed. published by Faith Press, London.

———. "A Musical Study of the Hymns of Casia." *Byzantinische Zeitschrift* 20 (1911) pp. 420–85.

ENGLISH: LITURGICAL COLLECTIONS

Triodion

Savas, Savas J., trans. *The Treasury of Orthodox Hymnology: Triodion: An Historical and Hymnographic Examination.* Minneapolis: Light and Life, 1983.

Mary, Mother, and Kallistos Ware, trans. *The Lenten Triodion.* London and Boston: Faber and Faber, 1978 (Service Books of the Orthodox Church).

Menaion

Lambertsen, Isaac E., trans. *The Menaion of the Orthodox Church: Collected Services, together with Selected Akathist Hymns.* Liberty, Tenn.: St. John of Kronstadt Press (Rt. 1, Box 205, Liberty, TN 37095), 1987.

Mary, Mother, and Kallistos Ware, trans. *The Festal Menaion.* London: Faber, 1977 (Service Books of the Orthodox Church).

Orloff, Nicolas, trans. *The General Menaion; or, The Book of Services Common to the Festivals of Our Lord Jesus of the Holy Virgin and of the Different Orders of Saints.* Bloomington, Ill: n. p.; Leiden: Brill, 1984. Reprint of the 1899 ed.

GERMAN (AND GREEK)

Homeyer, Helene, trans. *Dichterinnen des Altertums und des frühen Mittelalters.* Paderborn: Schöningh, 1979.

GREEK

Koutloumousianos, Vartholomaios, ed. *Menaion periechon hapasan ten anekousan auto akolouthian.* Venice, 1843.

Krumbacher, K. "Kasia." In *Sitzungsberichte der philsophisch-philologischen und der historischen Classe der k.b[ayrische]. Akademie der Wissenschaften.* 1897, pp. 305–70.

Papadopoulos, N. P. "Kassianes hymnoi." *Hoi Treis hierarchai* vol. 47, 1956, pp. 2f., 22f., 26f., 36, 45f., 53, 62f., 70f., 74f., 87f., 92–94; vol. 48, 1957, 6f., 13f.

Papadopoulos-Kerameneus, A. "Analekta Ierosolumnitikes Stachuologias, 2." *En Petroupolei*, 1894.

Petrides, S. "Cassia." *Revue de l'orient chrétien* 7 (1902) pp. 218–44.

Trempelas, P. N. *Ekloge ellenikes orthodoxou hymnographias.* Athens, 1949 (Vivliotheke apostolikes diakonias 20).

Tzedakes, Th. B. "Kassiane he megale tes ekklesias melodos." *Apostolos Titos (Deltion tes hieras metropoleos Kretes)* vol. 8 (1959) pp. 72–74, 92–95, 107–9; vol. 9 (1960) pp. 211–15; vol. 10 (1961) pp. 8–10, 53–56, 94–96, 129–33, 154f., 177f., 197f., 214–17; vol. 11 (1962) pp. 14f., 30–32, 48–50, 88–91, 153–56, 175–77, 195–98, 217–20; vol. 12 (1963) pp. 6–9, 36f., 52–55, 73–76.

Thekla the Nun (ninth century)

Thekla was probably an abbess in ninth-century Constantinople. All that is really known of her is her one surviving poem, an encomium to the Theotokos (Virgin Mary). Thekla, like Kassiane and Theodosia, lived in a time when women were essential in the effective opposition to the iconoclasts who had achieved ascendancy in the previous century.

FOR DISCUSSION OF THEKLA'S LIFE AND WRITINGS

Topping, Eva Catafygiotu. "Thekla the Nun: In Praise of Woman." *Greek Orthodox Theological Review* 25 (1980) pp. 353–70. This contains about half the verses of the poem in Greek as well as analysis of the poem.

GREEK

Nikodemos, Monachos ho Naxios. *Theotokarion: Neon poikilon kai horaiotaton oktoechon.* Volos, 1949, pp. 34–37.

Eustratiades, Sophronios. *Theotokarion A.* Chennevieressur-Marne, 1931, pp. 166–68.

Theodosia

FOR DISCUSSION OF THEODOSIA AND HER WRITINGS

Topping, Eva Catafygiotu. "Make a Joyful Noise! Women Hymnographers of Byzantium." In *Holy Mothers of Orthodoxy.* Minneapolis: Light and Life, 1987, pp. 83–94.

———. "Theodosia: Melodos and monastria." *Diptycha* 4 (1986–87) pp. 384–405.

———. "Women Hymnographers in Byzantium." *Diptycha* 3 (1982–83) pp. 98–111.

Syrian Saints

Few sources have come down to us for the life and thought of women of the Christian churches of the East, beyond the Byzantine Empire. The excerpts listed below would normally be outside the scope of this work because they are hagiography written by men with no real sense of incorporating autobiographical testimonies of women. However, these are the most likely to be firsthand accounts of what was done and said by actual women from Syriac-speaking Christianity in the first few centuries.

Mary and Euphemia

John of Ephesus. "Mary and Euphemia." In Sebastian P. Brock and Susan Ashbrook Harvey, *Holy Women of the Syrian Orient: The Transformation of the Classical Heritage.* Berkeley: University of California Press, 1987, pp. 122–33.

Susan

John of Ephesus. "Susan." In Sebastian P. Brock and Susan Ashbrook Harvey, *Holy Women of the Syrian Orient,* pp. 133–41.

Shirin–Martyrius (Sahalona)

"Shirin–Martyrius (Sahalona)." In Sebastian P. Brock and Susan Ashbrook Harvey, *Holy Women of the Syrian Orient,* pp. 177–81.

Women Martyrs of Najran

"Women Martyrs of Najran." In Sebastian P. Brock and Susan Ashbrook Harvey, *Holy Women of the Syrian Orient,* pp. 100–121.

Armenian Hymnographers

The two poets listed below wrote hymns for the liturgy of Armenia, celebrating the lives of saints of the oriental church. At the present time, no translation into English is available.

FOR DISCUSSION OF THESE AUTHORS

Inglisian, Vahan. In Gerhard Deeters, "Die armenische Literatur." *Armenisch und kaukasische Sprachen.* Leiden and Cologne: Brill, 1963 (Handbuch der Orientalistik 1; Der Nahe und der Mittlere Osten 7) p. 176.

Khosrovidukht

Khosrovidukht was the daughter of Prince Khosrov Goght'nac'i and sister of the martyr Vahan of Goghtn, who died in 737. Her hymn for his feast day is extraordinary for its directness and the quality of its affect.

Acharian, Hracheay. *Hayots' andznanunnerri bararan* (Armenian prosopographical dictionary). Erevan: Petakan Hamalsarani Hratarakchutyun, 1942–62; Beirut: Sevan Press, 1972, 2:539–40.

Hakobyan, Grigor A., et al., eds. *Margaritner hay k'narergut'yun* (Pearls of Armenian lyric). Erevan: Hayastan Press, 1971, p. 51.

Sahakdukht

Sahakdukht was a composer of hymns and their melodies. She came from a prominent ecclesiastical family. She became a nun in her youth and lived a life of solitary asceticism in a cave in the valley near Garni. There she had various pupils whom she instructed from behind a curtain. One of her poems can be clearly identified as hers because her name appears in an acrostic, but other texts by her may survive anonymously in the Armenian liturgy.

Hakobyan, Grigor A., et al., eds. *Margaritner hay k'narergut'yun* (Pearls of Armenian lyric). Erevan: Hayastan Press, 1971, pp. 49–50.

Pogharian, Norayr. *Hay groghner* (Armenian writers). Jerusalem: Tparan Srbots Hakobeants (St. James Press), 1971, pp. 116–18.

Anna Comnena (1083–1153)

Anna was the daughter of Emperor Alexius I Comnenus and Irene. She retired to a convent after she and her husband failed to win control of the Byzantine Empire from her brother, John, after her father's death. She wrote the *Alexiad* about her father's reign. It is a panegyric or apology rather than a critical history. Though it always takes Alexius's part, it is valuable in understanding the attitudes of the Orthodox Christians to Western Europeans at the time of the crusades.

Alexiad

ENGLISH

Sewter, Edgar Robert Ashton, trans. *The Alexiad of Anna Comnena.* Baltimore: Penguin, 1969.

Dawes, Elizabeth A. S., trans. *The Alexiad of the Princess Anna Comnena, Being the History of the Reign of Her Father, Alexius I, Emperor of the Romans, 1081–1118 A.D.* London: Kegan Paul, Trench, Trübner, 1928. Reprints: New York: Barnes and Noble, 1967; New York: AMS, 1978.

SELECTIONS

"A Byzantine Historian of the First Crusade: Anna Comnena." In Marcelle Thiébaux, trans., *The Writings of Medieval Women,* pp. 91–104; 2d ed., pp. 225–39.

Sewter, E. R. A., trans. "Anna Comnena — The Alexiad." In Serinity Young, ed., *An Anthology of Sacred Texts by and about Women,* p. 59.

FRENCH AND GREEK

Impellizzeri, Salvatore. *La precrociata di Roberto il Guiscardo: Pagine dall'Alessiade.* Bari: Dedalo, 1965. Greek text and French translation on opposite pages.

Leib, Bernard, ed. and trans. *Alexiade (Règne de l'Empereur Alexis I Comnène, 1081–1118).* Paris: Société d'Édition "Les Belles Lettres," 1937; reprint, 1967. French and Greek on opposite pages.

GREEK

Hunger, Herbert. *Anonyme Metaphrase zu Anna Komnene, Alexias XI–XIII: Ein Beitrag zur Erschliessung der byzantinischen Umgangssprache.* Vienna: Verlag der Österreichischen Akademie der

Wissenschaften, 1981 (Wiener byzantinistische studien 15). Text in classical Greek and modern Greek.

Reifferscheid, August, ed. *Annae Comnenae, Porphyrogenitae, Alexias.* Leipzig: B. G. Teubner, 1884 (Bibliotheca scriptorum graecorum et romanorum teubneriana).

Acominatus, Nicetas Choniates. *Recueil des historiens des croisades: Historiens grecs.* Ed. Alexandre Hase and E. Miller. Paris: Imprimerie Nationale, 1875. Text in Greek or Latin.

Schopen, Ludwig, et al., eds. *Annae Comnenae Alexiadis libri XV.* Bonn: Weber, 1839, vol. 2, bks. 10-15. Greek and Latin.

POLISH

Jurewicz, Oktawiusz S., ed. *Aleksjada Z jezyka greckiego przelozyl. wstepem i przypisami opat rzyl Oktawiusz Jurewicz.* Wroclaw: Zaklad Narodowy im. Ossolinskich, 1969.

RUSSIAN

Liubarskii, I. A. N., trans. *Aleksiada.* Moscow: Nauka; Glav. Red. Vostochnoi Lit-ry, 1965.

MODERN GREEK

Alexias. Athens: Ekdoseis Agra, [1990–]. Translation based on the French edition: *Alexiade (Règne de l'Empereur Alexis I Comnène, 1081–1118).*

Irene Eulogia Choumnaina Palaiologos (1291–1355)

Eulogia was the widow, at an early age, of Despot John Palaiologos, son of Emperor Andronikos II. She came from a wealthy family that was much involved in the intellectual and political life of the Byzantine Empire. She became an abbess and used her money and influence against John Palaiologos and his disciples in the Hesychast controversy. The texts that we have from her are private letters that have been found in a single manuscript. These document her correspondence with a young monk, in an effort to persuade him to become her spiritual director.

GREEK AND ENGLISH

Hero, Angela Constantinides. *A Woman's Quest for Spiritual Guidance: The Correspondence of Princess Irene Eulogia Choumnaina Palaiologos.* Brookline, Mass.: Hellenic College Press, 1986 (Archbishop Iakovos Library of Ecclesiastical and Historical Sources 10).

Chapter 4

Western Europe in the Eighth through Tenth Centuries

The Circle of Saint Boniface (680–754)

The English (Anglo-Saxon) "apostle to Germany" maintained a correspondence that survives. There are several letters from abbesses and other nuns (most of them in England) to Boniface and to others. Only the writings of women are listed here, but correspondence to these women and others is also in these sources. The bibliography for this correspondence is listed after the writers.

Aelffled (eighth century)

Letter to Adola. Tangl, letter 8 (pp. 3–4); Unterkircher, fols. 34v–35r.

Berthgyth (eighth century)

Letters to Balthard. Tangl, letters 143, 147, 148 (pp. 282, 284–87); Unterkircher, fols. 33v, 34v–35v.

Bugga (eighth century)

To Boniface. Tangl, letter 15 (pp. 26–28); Unterkircher, fols. 20v–21r; Talbot, letter 4 (pp. 69–70); Emerton, letter 7, pp. 40–41.

Eangyth, Bugga (eighth century)

To Boniface. Tangl, letter 14 (pp. 21–26); Unterkircher, fols. 21v–23v; Emerton, letter 6, pp. 36–40.

Egburg (eighth century)

To Boniface. Tangl, letter 13 (pp. 18–21); Unterkircher, fols. 64r–65r; Emerton, letter 5, pp. 34–36.

Hugeburc (Huneberc) of Heidenheim (eighth century)

"Vita Willibaldi Episcopi Eichstetensis." *Monumenta germaniae historica:* Scriptores 15/1, pp. 86–106.

Talbot, C. H., trans. "The Hodoeporicon of St. Willibald." In Elizabeth Petroff, ed., *Medieval Women's Visionary Literature,* pp. 92–106.

"The Hodoeporicon of St. Willibald." In Talbot (see below), pp. 152–77.

"Vita Wynnebaldi Abbatis Heidenheimensis." *Monumenta germaniae historica:* Scriptores 15/1, pp. 106–17.

Leobgyda (Leoba) (eighth century)

To Boniface. Tangl, letter 29 (pp. 52–53); Unterkircher, fols. 21r–v; Talbot, letter 17 (pp. 87–88); Emerton, letter 21, pp. 59–60.

A translation of *The life of Saint Leoba* by Rudolf, a monk of Fulda, appears in Talbot (see below), 203–26.

"Vita Leobae abbatissae Biscofesheimensis auct. Rudolfo Fuldensi." *Monumenta germaniae historica:* Scriptores 15/1, pp. 118–31.

SOURCES

ENGLISH

Brownlow, William R. B., trans. *The Hodoeporicon of Saint Willibald.* London, 1891 (Palestine Pilgrims' Text Society Library 3/2); reprint: New York: AMS Press, 1971.

Talbot, Charles H., trans. and ed. *The Anglo-Saxon Missionaries in Germany.* London and New York: Sheed and Ward, 1954 (The Makers of Christendom). Contains "the lives of SS. Willibrord, Boniface, Sturm, Leoba and Lebuin, together with the *Hodoeporicon* of St. Willibald and a selection from the correspondence of St. Boniface."

Emerton, Ephraim, trans., and George La Piana, ed. *The Letters of Saint Boniface.* New York: Columbia University Press, 1940 (Records of Civilization; Sources and Studies 31); revision by George La Piana; reprint, New York: Octagon Books, 1973.

Kylie, Edward Joseph. *The English Correspondence of Saint Boniface: Being for the Most Part Letters Exchanged between the Apostle of the Germans and His English Friends.* London: Chatto and Windus, 1911; reprint: New York: Cooper Square, 1966.

SELECTIONS

"Barbarian Women, Holy Women: *The Wife's Lament; Wulf and Eadwacer; Leoba of England and Germany.*" In Marcelle Thiébaux, trans., *The Writings of Medieval Women,* 2d ed., pp. 135–52.

Talbot, C. H., trans. "Leoba, *Life of Saint Leoba.*" In Amy G. Oden, ed., *In Her Words: Women's Writings in the History of Christian Thought,* pp. 87–93.

CRITICAL EDITIONS

Tangl, Michael. *Die Briefe des heiligen Bonifatius und Lullus.* Berlin: Weidmann, 1916 (Monumenta germaniae historica: Epistolae selectae 1). Reprints, Munich: Monumenta Germaniae Historica, 1978; New York: Johnson Reprint, 1965. Text in Latin; introduction in German.

Unterkircher, Franz. *Sancti Bonifacii epistolae.* Graz: Akademische Druck- und Verlagsanstalt, 1971 (Codices selecti phototypice impressi 24).

Waitz, Georg, ed. *Vita Leobae abbatissae Biscofesheimensis auct. Rudolfo Fuldensi.* In *Monumenta germaniae historicae.* Hannover: Hahn, 1888 (Scriptorum [supplement] 15/2).

Holder-Egger, Oswald, ed. "Vita Willibaldi et Wynnebaldi auct. moniali Heidenheimensi." In *Monumenta germaniae historicae.* Hannover: Hahn, 1888 (Scriptorum [supplement] 15/2).

OTHER EDITIONS

Rau, Reinhold, and Presbyter Willibald. *Briefe des Bonifatius; Willibalds Leben des Bonifatius, nebst einigen zeitgenössischen Dokumenten. Unter Benützung der übersetzungen.* Darmstadt: Wissenschaftliche Buchgesellschaft, 1968 (Ausgewählte Quellen zur deutschen Geschichte der Mittelalters 4b). Latin and German.

Gisla (Abbess of Chelles) and
Rotruda (Daughter of Charlemagne)

Letter to Alcuin after April 19, 800

Allott, Stephen. *Alcuin of York, c. A.D. 732 to 804: His Life and Letters.* York: William Sessions Ltd., 1974. "The text used is that of E. Dümmler, Monumenta germaniae historica, Epistolae vol. IV."

Dümmler, Ernst, ed. *Monumenta germaniae historica.* Berlin: Weidmann, 1895 (Epistolarum 4; Karolini Aevi 2), letter 196, pp. 323–24.

Imma

Letters to Her Husband, Einhard (828–36)

Hampe, Karl, ed. *Monumenta germaniae historica.* Berlin: Weidmann, 1899 (Epistolarum 5; Karolini Aevi 3) pp. 128–29.

Bertha of Tuscany (tenth century)

Bertha of Tuscany was a member of the Italian aristocracy who wrote letters to Caliph Muktafi that are still extant in Arabic.

Levi della Vida, G., trans. "La corrispondenza di Berta di Toscana col Califfo Muktafi." *Rivista storica italiana* 66 (1954) pp. 21–38.

Liadain (ninth century?)

Comracc Líadaine Cuirithir

This poem is the story of a love affair between a woman and a man who are poets. At the end of the story, Liadain decides to become a nun. There is no consensus whether the poem or Liadain's portions of the poetic dialogue was written by a woman, but it is possible.

ENGLISH

Saul, George Brandon, trans. *Liadain and Curithir: A Medieval Irish Love Story, and Four Tales from the Elf-Mounds*. Philadelphia: Walton Press, 1970.

Fox, Moireen. *Liadain and Curithir*. Oxford: B. H. Blackwell, 1917.

IRISH (GAELIC) AND ENGLISH

Meyer, Kuno, ed. and trans. *Liadain and Curithir, an Irish Love-Story of the Ninth Century*. London: D. Nutt, 1902.

Dhuoda (ninth century)

Dhuoda was married to a nobleman who was deeply involved in the political and military struggles that followed the death of Charlemagne. She was virtually abandoned and placed on an estate in Uzes, far from her original home. As a consequence of her husband's political problems, he took away her two sons to give as hostages. Dhuoda wrote her manual of religious, practical, and political advice to her older son because this separation made it impossible for her to see him or help him otherwise.

ENGLISH

Neel, Carol. *Handbook for William: A Carolingian Woman's Counsel for Her Son*. Lincoln: University of Nebraska Press, 1991 (Regents Studies in Medieval Culture). Includes bibliographical references (pp. 147–52).

SELECTIONS

"A Carolingian Mother: Dhuoda." In Marcelle Thiébaux, trans., *The Writings of Medieval Women*, pp. 65–79.

"Dhuoda." In Helene Homeyer, trans., *Dichterinnen des Altertums und des frühen Mittelalters*, pp. 188–201

"Dhuoda." In Peter Dronke, *Women Writers of the Middle Ages*, pp. 36–54 (excerpts).

Marchand, James, trans. "Dhuoda, *Manual (841)*." In Amy G. Oden, ed., *In Her Words: Women's Writings in the History of Christian Thought,* pp. 94–98.

————. "The Frankish Mother: Dhuoda." In Katharina M. Wilson, ed., *Medieval Women Writers,* pp. 1–29.

"A Mother to a Young Warrior: Dhuoda of Uzès." In Marcelle Thiébaux, trans., *The Writings of Medieval Women,* 2d ed., pp. 153–70.

LATIN AND FRENCH

Riché, Pierre. *Manuel pour mon fils.* Paris: Cerf, 1975 (Sources chrétiennes 225); 2d ed., 1991.

Bondurand, Edouard Bligny. *L' éducation carolingienne: Le manuel de Dhuoda (843).* Paris, 1887; also Geneva: Megariotis Reprints, 1978. Latin text and French translation.

LATIN AND GERMAN

Strecker, Karl, ed. *Poeti latini aevi carolini.* Berlin: Weidmann, 1923 (Monumenta germaniae historica: Poetarum latinorum medii aevi 4, fasc. 2) pp. 703–17.

Meier, Gabriel. *Ausgewählter Schriften von Columen, Alkuin, Dodana...* Freiburg, 1890 (Bibliothek der katholischer Pädogogik 3).

Erdmann, Oskar, ed. *Otfrids Evangelienbuch.* Tübingen: M. Niemeyer, 1957 (Altdeutsche Textbibliothek 49). Reprint of 1882 ed.

ITALIAN AND LATIN

Biffi, Inos. *Educare nel medioevo: Per la formazione di mio figlio: Manuale.* Milan: Jaca Book, 1984, 1982 (Biblioteca di cultura medievale). Latin text with Italian translation, introduction in Italian.

Aethelgifu (tenth century)

Aethelgifu was a wealthy Anglo-Saxon matron who owned property, including slaves. The manuscript copy of her will survives and has been published. The contents of her substantial estate and the way in which she controlled it and disposed of it in her will are of interest.

FOR EXPLANATION OF ANGLO-SAXON WILLS AND DISCUSSION OF
AETHELGIFU'S WILL

Whitelock, Dorothy. *Anglo-Saxon Wills.* Holmes Beach, Fla.: Gaunt,
1986.

TEXT

Whitelock, Dorothy, and Francis James Rennell Rodd. *The Will of
Aethelgifu: A Tenth-century Anglo-Saxon Manuscript.* Oxford: Oxford University Press, 1968. Includes a facsimile of the will.

Icelandic Women Poets

There are a number of brief poems by women that can be found
among the Icelandic sagas and *eddas.* It is interesting to note
that most of the poems that can most reliably be attributed to
women authors date from before the coming of Christianity to
Iceland in 980. In fact the verses by Steinunn Refsdóttir record
an excerpt from her debate against a Christian missionary. The
largest amount of Icelandic poetry attributed to women is assigned
to legendary women of the distant past. Sandra Straubhaar asks
(p. 4): "Was it easier for the medieval Icelander to imagine more
dynamic women skald figures in 'ancient times' because there
had been in fact more of them in some prehistoric period...?"
Since the sagas remain important in the culture of Christian Iceland, the negative correlation between Christianity and women's
authorship is interesting enough to justify the inclusion of the
texts of the most well-authenticated authors. The numbers refer
to pages where text and translation appear in Sandra Straubhaar's
dissertation.

Hildr Hrólfsdóttir Nefju (c. 900)   p. 12

Jórunn Skálmær
(early tenth century)   pp. 25, 27, 29, 30, 33, 34

ENGLISH AND OLD ICELANDIC

Straubhaar, Sandra Ballif. "Critical Notes on the Old Icelandic Skáldkonur." Ph.D. diss., Stanford University, 1982. Available from
University Microfilms International.

ICELANDIC AND OLD ICELANDIC

GuÐún P. Helgadóttir. *Skáldkonur fyrri alda.* 2 vols. Akureyri: Kvóldvó-
kuútgáfan, 1961–63.

Hrotsvit of Gandersheim (tenth century)

A canoness in a prosperous and influential community of women
that had connections with the court, Hrotsvit wrote a number of
plays and accounts of the lives of saints. Hrotsvit is one of the
most popular early medieval writers. Some of her plays have been
produced in modern productions.

LIST OF PLAYS

The Conversion of the Harlot Thais (or: *Paphnutius*)
The Resurrection of Drusiana and Calimachus (or: *Calimachus*)
The Conversion of General Gallicanus (or: *Gallicanus*)
The Martyrdom of the Holy Maids Faith, Hope, and Charity (or:
Sapientia)

The Martyrdom of the Holy Virgins Agape, Chiona, and Hirene (or: *Dulcitius*)
The Fall and Repentance of Mary the Niece of Abraham (or: *Abraham*)

LIST OF LEGENDS (LIVES OF SAINTS)

Mary	Dionysius	Theophilus	Gongolf
Pelagius	Ascension	Agnes	Basilius

SELECTIONS

"A Convent in Saxony: Hrotswitha of Gandersheim." In Marcelle Thié-baux, trans., *The Writings of Medieval Women,* pp. 81–104.

"Hagiographer, Playwright, Epic Historian: Hrotswitha of Gander-sheim." In Marcelle Thiébaux, trans., *The Writings of Medieval Women,* 2d ed., pp. 171–223.

Wilson, Katharina M., trans. "Abraham." In Elizabeth Petroff, ed., *Medieval Women's Visionary Literature,* pp. 124–35.

———. "Hrotsvit of Gandersheim, *Dulcitius.*" In Amy G. Oden, ed., *In Her Words: Women's Writings in the History of Christian Thought,* pp. 99–106.

———. "Pelagius." In Elizabeth Petroff, ed., *Medieval Women's Vision-ary Literature,* pp. 114–24.

———. "The Saxon Canoness: Hrotsvit of Gandersheim." In Katharina M. Wilson, ed., *Medieval Women Writers,* pp. 30–63.

WORKS

LATIN

Strecker, Karl. *Hrotsvithae opera.* Leipzig: B.G. Teubneri, 1906, 1930 (Bibliotheca scriptorum graecorum et romanorum teubneriana).

Winterfeld, Paul von, ed. <*Hrotsvithae*> *opera recensvit et emendavit Pavlvs de Winterfeld.* Berlin: Weidmann, 1902 (Scriptores rerum germanicarum in usum scholarum ex monumentis germaniae his-toricis separatim editi). Reprint, Munich: Monumenta Germaniae Historica, 1978.

Patrologia cursus completus, series latina. Vol. 137. Paris: J.-P. Migne, 1879.

GERMAN

Homeyer, Helene, ed. *Hrotsvitha von Gandersheim Werke in Deutscher übertragung, mit einem Beitrag zur frühmittelalterlichen Dichtung.* Munich: Schöningh, 1973; earlier editions 1970, 1936.

Barack, Karl August, ed. *Die Werke der Hrotsvitha.* Nuremberg: Bauer und Raspe, 1858.

PLAYS

ENGLISH

Wilson, Katharina M., trans. *The Plays of Hrotsvit of Gandersheim.* New York: Garland, 1989 (Garland Library of Medieval Literature 62B).

————. *Plays: The dramas of Hrotsvit of Gandersheim.* Saskatoon: Peregrina, 1985 (Matrologia latina).

Bonfante, Larissa. *The Plays of Hrotswitha of Gandersheim.* New York: New York University Press, 1979.

St. John, Christopher, trans. *The Plays of Roswitha.* London: Chatto and Windus, 1923; reprint, New York: B. Blom, 1966.

Tillyard, H. J. W., trans. *The Plays of Roswitha.* Charing Cross: Faith Press, 1923.

OTHER LANGUAGES

Bertini, Ferruccio. *Dialoghi drammatici.* 1st ed. Milan: Garzanti, 1986. Latin text, parallel Italian translation. Includes bibliographies.

Magnin, Charles, trans. *Théatre de Hrotsvitha, religieuse allemande du 10ème siècle.* Paris: Duprat, 1845.

INDIVIDUAL PLAYS

Abraham

Lambert, Richard Stanton, trans., and Agnes Lambert, illus. *Abraham: A Play.* Wembly Hill, Middlesex: Stanton Press, 1922.

Langosch, Karl. *Dulcitius. Abraham. 2 Dramen.* Stuttgart: Philipp Reclam Jun, [1967].

Dulcitius

Adams, Joseph Q., ed. and trans. *Dulcitius: A Mediaeval Comedy.* Elmira, N.Y., 1916. ("Privately printed.") Photocopy available from University Microfilms International, 1980 (Ann Arbor, Mich.).

Paphnutius

Camden, Charles Carroll, trans. "Hrotswitha's Paphnutius." Master's thesis, University of Iowa, 1928.
Paphnutius: Comedie de Hrotsvitha. Paris: "Mercure de France," 1895.

Calimachus

Hacks, Peter, and Johann Wolfgang von Goethe. *Das Jahrmarktsfest zu Plundersweilern; Rosie traumt.* 2d ed. Berlin: Aufbau-Verlag, 1982.
Calímaco. Monterrey: Ediciones Sierra Madre, 1969. Parallel text in Latin and Spanish.

POETRY

Sämtliche Dichtungen (Vollständige Ausg.). Munich: Winkler, 1966.
Gundlach, Wilhelm, ed. and trans., and Carmen de bello Saxonico and Oscar Doering, trans. *Heldenlieder der deutschen Kaiserzeit aus dem Lateinischen übersetzt, an zeitgenössischen Berichten erläutert...* 3 vols. Innsbruck: Wagner, 1894–99.
Pfund, Theodor Gottfried Martin, trans., and Wilhelm Wattenbach, ed. *Carmen de primordiis coenobii gandersheimensis and Carmen de gestis Oddonis I. imperatoris Der Hrotsuitha Gedicht über Gandersheims Gründung und die thaten kaiser Oddo I. Nach der ausgabe der Monumenta Germaniae übersetzt von dr Th.* 2d ed. Leipzig: Dyk, 1891.
Pfund, Theodor Gottfried Martin. *Der Hrotsuitha Gedicht über Gandersheims Gründing und die Thaten Kaiser Oddo I.* Berlin: W. Besser, 1860.

OTHER WORKS

Knauer, Helmut. *Legenden.* Stuttgart: J. C. Mellinger, 1964.
Wiegand, Gonsalva, ed. and trans. "The Non-dramatic Works of Hrosvitha: Text, Translation, and Commentary." Ph.D. diss., St. Louis University, 1936.

Chapter 5 _____

Eleventh and Twelfth Centuries: Poets and Benedictines

Personal Poetry

Constance

Constance was a young nun from Angers in France whose letter in verse in reply to a verse letter from Baudri of Bourgueil (Baldricus, archbishop of Dol) appears in his works. Nothing is known of her except for that which can be gleaned from the correspondence itself. For discussion, see Peter Dronke, *Women Writers of the Middle Ages,* pp. 84–91.

Hilbert, Karlheinz, ed. and trans. *Baldricus Burgulianus Carmina.* Heidelberg: Winter, 1979 (Editiones Heidelbergenses 19) pp. 158–70. Text in Latin with notes in German.

Carmina ratisponensia (eleventh century, second half)

This manuscript from the area of Regensburg in Germany is a "magnificent chaos" — a variety of texts from different sources mixed together. Within this collection can be found approximately thirty brief poems by young women. The identity of the writer or writers is unknown, but they address a *magister* who was a teacher or director of lay pupils or nuns.

Dronke, Peter. *Medieval Latin and the Rise of European Love-Lyric.* 2d ed. Oxford: Clarendon, 1968. "The Love Verses from Regensburg," text and translation are in 2:422–47; discussion in 1:221–29.
Paravicini, A., ed. *Carmina ratisponensia.* Heidelberg, 1979.

Epistolae duorum amantium

These letters in rhymed prose and verse have sometimes been attributed to Abelard and Héloïse. Recently scholars have tended to believe that they are by another pair of lovers who resemble Abelard and Héloïse in education and sophistication.

Könsgen, Ewald, ed. *Epistolae duorum amantium Briefe Abaelards und Heloises?* Leiden: Brill, 1974 (Mittellateinische Studien und Texte, 8/8).

Visio cuiusdam pauperculae mulieris

Houben, H., ed. "Visio cuiusdam pauperculae mulieris." *Zeitschrift für die Geschichte des Oberrheins* 124 (1976) pp. 31–42.

Tergensee Love Letters

Within this collection are an exchange of several love poems between a woman and a man. Peter Dronke has argued that these poems are by two actual lovers.

Dronke, Peter. *Medieval Latin and the Rise of European Love-lyric.* 2d ed. Oxford: Clarendon, 1968. Text and translation are in 2:472–82.
Strecker, Karl, ed. *Monumenta germaniae historica. Codex epistolarum tegernseensium (Froumund) = Die Tegernseer Briefsammlung (Froumund).* Berlin: Weidmann, 1925 (Epistolae selectae 3).

Compiuta Donzella (late thirteenth century)

We have three poems by this woman from Florence.

Contini, Gianfranco, ed. *Poeti del duecento.* Milan: R. Ricciardi, 1960 (La letteratura italiana: Storia e testi 2) 1:433–38; reprint, Torino: Einaudi, 1977.

Trotula (eleventh century)

Nothing is known about the author of this medieval treatise on women's health. It is debated whether the feminine name "Trotula" is the actual name of a person or whether it is derived from a somewhat pejorative term meaning "old crone." The treatise comes from Italy in the eleventh century, probably Salerno, and contains instructions for gynecological diagnosis and treatment. See the introduction to Beryl Rowland's translation.

ENGLISH

Rowland, Beryl. *Medieval Woman's Guide to Health: The First English Gynecological Handbook*. Kent, Ohio: Kent State University Press, 1981.

Hallaert, M. R. *The "Sekenesse of Wymmen": A Middle English Treatise on Diseases in Women*. Brussels: Omirel, UFSAL, 1982. (Yale Medical Library, MS 47, fols. 60r–71v).

Mason-Hohl, Elizabeth. *The Diseases of Women by Trotula of Salerno: A Translation of "Passionibus mulierum curandorum."* New York: Ward Ritchie Press, 1940.

FLEMISH

Delva, Anna Blanca Césarine Maria. *Vrouwengeneeskunde in Vlaanderen tijdens de late middeleeuwen: Met uitgave van het Brugse Liber Trotula*. Bruges: A. Delva en het Genootschap voor Geschiedenis Thesis (doctoral) — Rijksuniversiteit te Leiden, 1983 (Vlaamse historische studies 2). With a French summary.

ITALIAN

Cavallo Boggi, Pina. *Sulle malattie delle donne*. Torino: Edizioni La Rosa, 1979.

Constance of Sicily (1154–98)

Constance was the daughter of Roger II, king of Sicily. She ruled Sicily and married Henry VI of Germany, the Holy Roman emperor. Their son was three years old when Henry died in 1197, and Constance was in a strong position in the regency government for her son when she died a year later. A substantial volume of her official papers relating to government and diplomacy is published in the series Monumenta Germaniae Historica.

Kölzer, Theo., ed. *Die Urkunden der Kaiserin Konstanze = Constantiae imperatricis diplomata*. Hannover: Hahn, 1990 (Monumenta germaniae historica; Diplomata regum et imperatorum germaniae 11, pt. 3 = Monumenta germaniae historica; Die Urkunden des deutschen Könige und Kaiser 11/3).

Mathilde, Countess of Morit (twelfth century)

Letter to Abbot Rupert of Tergensee (1166)

Sandberger, G. ed. *Der Schlern* 52 (1978) pp. 503–9.

Ava of Melk (d. 1127)

Ava wrote religious poetry recounting several biblical and religious events. She was a widow in Austria and had several children who helped her with writing and understanding these events.

ENGLISH

Moehs, Teta E. *The Gospel of Jesus Christ according to Mistress Ava*. New York: Senda Nueva de Ediciones, 1986 (Senda de estudios y ensayos). English and modern German from the edition of Friedrich Maurer.

CRITICAL EDITION

Schacks, Kurt. *Die Dichtungen der Frau Ava*. Graz: Akademische Druck- u. Verlagsanstalt, 1986 (Wiener Neudrucke 8). Text in Middle High German with commentary in German.

CONCORDANCE

Schacks, Kurt. *Lemmatisierte Konkordanz zu den Dichtungen der Frau Ava*. Bern and New York: Peter Lang, 1991.

GERMAN

Maurer, Friedrich, ed. *Die Dichtungen der Frau Ava*. Tübingen: Niemeyer, 1966 (Altdeutsche Textbibliothek 66)

Trobairitz

Among the troubadour songs from twelfth- and thirteenth-century Provence, twenty texts survive that were written by women.

Castelloza (thirteenth century)

Bogin, pp. 118–29.
Schultz-Gora, 23, 24.
Dronke, Peter, trans. "The Provençal Trobairitz: Castelloza." In Katharina M. Wilson, ed., *Medieval Women Writers*, pp. 131–52.

Garsenda (thirteenth century)

Bogin, pp. 108–9.
Schultz-Gora, 21 [4].

H (Domna) (thirteenth century)

Bogin, pp. 138–43.
Schultz-Gora, 25 [12].

Lombarda (thirteenth century)

Bogin, pp. 114–17.
Thiébaux, *The Writings of Medieval Women*, 2d ed., p. 258.
Boutière, Schutz, and Cluzel, pp. 417f.
Véran, Jules. *Les poetesses provençales du moyen âge et de nos jours*. Paris: Librairie Aristide Quillet, 1946, p. 90.

Maria de Ventadorn (thirteenth century)

Bogin, pp. 98–101.
Schultz-Gora, 21.

Audiau, Jean, ed. *Les poésies des quatre troubadours d'Ussel.* Paris: Delagrave, 1922, no. 15.

Tibors (eleventh century)

Bogin, pp. 80–81.
Thiébaux, *The Writings of Medieval Women,* 2d ed., p. 256.
Schultz-Gora, 25.
Boutièrre, Schutz, and Cluzel, pp. 498f.
Dronke, *Women Writers of the Middle Ages,* p. 99 (trans.), p. 299 (text).

Anonymous

Bogin, pp. 146–51.
Schultz-Gora, 28–30 [I–IV].
Riquer, 1:452–54, 576f.

Alamanda (twelfth century)

Bogin, pp. 102–7.
Schultz-Gora, 19.
Kolsen, Adolf, ed. *Sämtliche lieder des trobadors Giraut de Bornelh.* Halle: Niemeyer, 1910–35, vol. 1, no. 57.

Comtessa de Dia

Bogin, pp. 82–91.
Thiébaux, *The Writings of Medieval Women,* pp. 183–91; 2d ed., pp. 265–70.
Schultz-Gora, 17, 18.
Dronke, *Women Writers of the Middle Ages,* p. 103 (trans.).
Riquer, 1:452–54; 2:791–802.

Almucs de Castelnau, Iseut de Capio

Bogin, pp. 92–93.
Thiébaux, *The Writings of Medieval Women,* p. 191; 2d ed., pp. 259–60.
Schultz-Gora, 25.

Dronke, *Women Writers of the Middle Ages,* p. 100 (trans.), p. 300 (text).
Boutièrre, Schutz, and Cluzel, pp. 422–24.

Alais, Carenza, Yselda

Bogin, pp. 144–45.
Thiébaux, *The Writings of Medieval Women,* pp. 193–94; 2d ed., pp. 260–61.
Schultz-Gora, 28.
Dronke, *Women Writers of the Middle Ages,* pp. 101–2 (trans.), pp. 300–302 (text).

Beiris de Romans (thirteenth century)

Bogin, pp. 132–33.
Thiébaux, *The Writings of Medieval Women,* p. 192; 2d ed., p. 257.
Schultz-Gora, 28 [15].

Azalais Porcairagues (twelfth century)

Bogin, pp. 94–97.
Thiébaux, *The Writings of Medieval Women,* 2d ed., pp. 263–65.
Schultz-Gora, 16.
Riquer, 1:459–62.

Azelais d'Altier

Crescini, V. "Tanz salutz e tantas amors." *Zeitschrift für romanische Philologie* 14 (1890) pp. 128–32.

Germonda (thirteenth century)

Véran, Jules. *Les poetesses provençales du moyen age et de nos jours.* Paris: Librairie Aristide Quillet, 1946, pp. 194–219.

Clara d'Anduza

Bogin, pp. 130–31.
Schultz-Gora, 26 [13].

SOURCES

Bogin, Magda. *The Women Troubadours.* New York: Paddington Press, 1976; reprint, New York: Norton, 1980.

Bogin, Meg, and Jeanne Faure-Cousin. *Les femmes troubadours.* Paris: Denoël/Gonthier, 1978 (Collection femme). Translation of *The Women Troubadours.* Includes a selection of poems translated from Provençal by Jeanne Faure-Cousin.

Boutière, Jean, Alexander H. Schutz, and Irenée-Marcel Cluzel. *Biographies des troubadours: Textes provençaux des XIIIe et XIVe siècles.* 2d ed. Paris: Nizet, 1973.

Dronke, Peter. *Women Writers of the Middle Ages: A Critical Study of Texts from Perpetua (d. 203) to Marguerite Porete (d. 1310).* Cambridge and New York: Cambridge University Press, 1984.

Riquer, Martín. *Los trovadores: Historia literaria y textos.* Barcelona: Planeta, 1975; Ariel, 1983 (Ensayos planeta de lingüística y crítica literaria 36). Published in 1948 under title *La lírica de los trovadores.*

Schultz-Gora, Oscar. *Die provenzalischen Dichterinnen: Biographien und Texte nebst Anmer kungen und einer Einl.* Leipzig: G. Fock, 1888; Geneva: Slatkine Reprints, 1975. Also in microfilm: New Haven: Research Publications, 1976 (History of Women 3633).

"The *Trobairitz* in Love and Strife." In Marcelle Thiébaux, trans., *The Writings of Medieval Women,* 2d ed., pp. 241–76.

"The Women Troubadours: The Countess of Dia, Almuc de Castelnou and Iseut de Capio, Bieris de Romans, Alaisina, Iselda, and Carenza, Anonymous." In Marcelle Thiébaux, trans., *The Writings of Medieval Women,* pp. 181–96.

Herrad of Hohenburg (1125–95)

Herrad was the abbess of a convent near Landsberg in Alsatia (near Strasbourg). The convent was prosperous and a center of intellectual life. The one text that we have from Herrad and her community is a compilation or encyclopedia that is made up of excerpts from earlier texts joined together by glosses, some of which are in verse. The greatest interest in this book has been in the beautiful miniatures that illuminate the early manuscript that is perhaps the original.

ENGLISH

Straub, A., G. Keller, and Aristide D. Caratzas, eds. *Hortus deliciarum (Garden of delights)*. New Rochelle, N.Y.: Caratzas Brothers, 1977. Translated from the original complete ed. published in Strasbourg, 1901.

LATIN

Green, Rosalie B., T. Julian Brown, and Kenneth Levy. *Hortus deliciarum*. London: Warburg Institute; Leiden: Brill, 1979. Two chapters in French.

Gillen, Otto. *Hortus deliciarum*. Neustadt/Weinstrasse: Pfälzische Verlagsanstalt, 1979.

Christen, Auguste. *Le jardin des délices de l'Abbesse Herrade de Landsberg*. Colmar: Alsatia Paris, 1968.

Heinsius, Maria. *Der Paradiesgarten der Herrad von Landsberg: Ein Zeugnis mittelalterlicher Kultur und Geistesgeschichte im Elsass*. Colmar: Alsatia Verlag: 1968. Reproductions of miniatures from the twelfth-century manuscript known as *Hortus deliciarum*. Captions in French and German.

Hortus deliciarum, le "jardin des délices"; un manuscrit alsacien à miniatures du XIIe siècle. Strasbourg: Oberlin, 1945.

Rott, H. G., and G. Wild. *Hortus deliciarum: Der "Wonnen-Garten" der Herrad von Landesberg: Eine elsässische Bilderhandschrift aus dem 12. Jahrhundert*. Mülhausen, Elsass: Braun, 1944. Issued in portfolio.

Das Lustgärtlein der Herrad von Landsberg: Ein Spiegel der Hohenstaufenzeit im Elsass. Colmar: Alsatia Verlag, 1932.

Straub, A., and G. Keller. *Hortus deliciarum*. Strasbourg: Impr. Strasbourgeoise, en Commission chez Trübner, 1879. Issued in eleven parts.

Engelhardt, Christian Mortiz. *Hortus deliciarum: Ein Beitrag zur Geschichte der Wissenschaften, Litteratur, Kunst, Kleidung, Waffen und Sitten des Mittelalters*. Stuttgart: J. G. Cotta, 1818.

Héloïse (1101–65)

Héloïse was the niece of Canon Fulbert of Paris. She was a student of Peter Abelard, one of the leading philosophers and theologians of the eleventh century. Héloïse and Abelard had a love affair and, apparently, were secretly married. Héloïse's uncle was unhappy about this and had Abelard beaten and mutilated. Héloïse was in a convent and Abelard went to a monastery. Later, when Héloïse was abbess and Abelard an abbot, they wrote letters to one another. The letters by Héloïse reveal a sophisticated mind, capable of engaging in complex theological discourse. Thus, some earlier scholars doubted that she wrote them, instead attributing them to Abelard. Recent scholarship, however, has tended to accept Héloïse's authorship.

FOR A DISCUSSION OF HÉLOÏSE'S AUTHORSHIP

Dronke, Peter. *Women Writers of the Middle Ages,* pp. 107–43.

Radice, Betty, and Raymond Hawthorn. *Abelard and Héloïse: The Story of His Misfortunes, and the Personal Letters.* London: Folio Society, 1977.

Scott-Moncrieff, Charles Kenneth, trans. *The Letters of Abelard and Héloïse.* New York: Knopf, 1926; reprint, New York: Cooper Square, 1974.

"1722 Edition"

Pope, Alexander, trans., and John Hughes and James Ellis Wellington, eds. *Eloïsa to Abelard, with the Letters of Héloïse to Abelard in the Version by John Hughes, 1713.* Coral Gables, Fla.: University of Miami Press, 1965. (University of Miami Critical Studies 5).

Pope, Alexander, and John Hughes, trans. *The Love Letters of Abelard and Héloïse.* New York: G. P. Putnam's Sons, 1905.

The Love Letters of Abelard and Héloïse; Tr. from the Original Latin and Now Reprinted from the Edition of 1722; Together with a Brief Account of Their Lives and Work. Indianapolis: Bobbs-Merrill, 1903.

Pope, Alexander, trans. *Letters of Abelard and Héloïse: With a Particular Account of Their Lives and Misfortunes. To Which Are Added, Poems by Pope, Madan, Cawthorne....* London: Newman, 1819.

Historia calamitatum

ENGLISH

Bellows, Henry Adams. *The Story of My Misfortunes: The Autobiography of Peter Abélard.* New York: Macmillan; London: Collier-Macmillan, 1972.

FRENCH

Monfrin, J. *Historia calamitatum.* Paris: Librairie philosophique J. Vrin, 1959.

FRENCH AND LATIN

Charrier, Charlotte, ed. *Jean de Meaun: Traduction de la première épître de Pierre Abélard (Historia calamitatum).* Paris: Librairie ancienne Honoré Champion, 1934. French and Latin on opposite pages.

GERMAN

Brost, Eberhard, trans. *Historia calamitatum Abaelard: Die Leidensgeschichte und der Briefwechsel mit Heloisa Eberhard Brost.* 4th ed. Heidelberg: Lambert Scheider, 1979.

Letters

FRENCH

Zumthor, Paul. *Correspondance.* Paris: Union Générale d'Éditions, 1983.

Oddoul, E. Edouard, and Jean Gigoux. *Lettres d'Abailard et d'Héloïse.* Plan de la Tour: Éditions d'Aujourd'hui, 1980.

Lettres. Paris: Union Générale d'Éditions, 1964.

Corot, Gilbert, trans. *Lettres d'Héloïse et d'Abélard.* Forcalquier, Haute Provence: R. Morel, 1963.

Lettres de Héloïse et Abélard. Paris: Mermod, 1950.

Oddoul, E. Edouard, trans. *Lettres d'Abailard et d'Héloïse.* Paris: E. Houdaille, 1839.

ITALIAN

Le lettere di Abelardo ed Eloisa. Torino: G. Einaudi, 1979.

de Meun, Jean, and Fabrizio Beggiato. *Le lettere di Abelardo ed Eloisa nella traduzione di Jean de Meun.* Modena: S.T.E.M. Mucchi, 1977. Text in Old French; introduction and notes in Italian.

Baumgärtner, P., trans. *Briefwechsel zwischen Abaelard und Héloïse.* Leipzig: P. Reclam, 1894.

Barbieri, Gaetano, and I. Gigoux. *Lettere di Abelardo ed Eloisa corredate di documenti antichi e moderni.* Milan: Andrea Ubicini, 1841.

Sankt Trudperter Hohes Lied (c. 1160)

This commentary on the Song of Songs was written for a community of Benedictine nuns at Admont, in the Steiermark region of Austria. It is among the earliest mystical texts written in the German language. The work is named for another monastery where the manuscript was discovered. The author of this commentary is unknown, and it is quite possible that a woman wrote it.

CRITICAL EDITION

Menhardt, Hermann, ed. *Das St. Trudperter Hohe Lied.* Halle: M. Niemeyer, 1934 (Rheinische Beiträge und Hülfsbücher zur germanischen Philologie und Volkskunde 21–22).

CONCORDANCE

Sauer-Geppert, Waldtraut-Ingeborg. *Wörterbuch zum St. Trudperter Hohen Lied: Ein Beitrag zur Sprache der mittelalterlichen Mystik.* Berlin and New York: De Gruyter, 1972 (Quellen und Forschungen zur Sprach- und Kulturgeschichte der germanischen Volker, n.s., 50 [174]).

Hildegard of Bingen (1098–1179)

Hildegard was one of the most influential women of her age and the most prolific of female medieval writers. She grew up under the care of a monastic recluse named Jutta. When Jutta died, Hildegard was her successor as abbess of the community that she had gathered. Several years later, the community moved to a large convent at Rupertsberg, near Bingen.

Hildegard had received visions and other extraordinary religious experiences from early childhood. After she was made abbess, she began to record her visions upon the advice of her confessor. This resulted in her *Scivias,* which gained her the reputation as a prophet and substantial influence in the church and the Holy Roman Empire of Frederick Barbarossa.

Hildegard also wrote copious material for the use of the monastic community: liturgical music, biblical commentary, compendia of natural science and healing, hagiography, and theological explanations of important formulas of the church.

AN INTRODUCTION TO HILDEGARD AND HER WORKS

Flanagan, Sabina. *Hildegard of Bingen, 1098–1179: A Visionary Life.* London and New York: Routledge, 1989.

A MAJOR ONGOING BIBLIOGRAPHY OF WORKS BY AND ABOUT HILDEGARD

Lauter, Werner. *Hildegard-Bibliographie: Wegweiser zur Hildegard-Literatur.* Alzey: Verlag der Rheinhessischen Druckwerkstätte, 1970–84 (Alzeyer Geschichtsblätter Sonderheft 4).

COMPLETE WORKS

Pitra, Jean Baptiste, ed. *Analecta sanctae Hildegardis opera spicilegio solesmensi parata.* Paris: A. Jouby et Roger, 1882 (Analecta sacra spicilegio parata 8); reprint, Farnborough: Gregg Press, 1966.

Migne, J. P., ed. *S. Hildegardis abbatissae opera omnia.* Paris: Garnier, 1882. Vol. 197 of *Patrologiae cursus completus, series latina.*

MINOR WORKS

Vita Sancti Disibodi
Vita Sancti Ruperti
Expositio evangeliorum
Explanatio symboli S. Athanasii
Explanatio regulae S. Benedicti
Lingua ignota; Litterae ignotae

COLLECTIONS OF HILDEGARD'S WORKS

Bowie, Fiona, and Davies, Oliver, eds. *Hildegard of Bingen: An Anthology.* London: SPCK, 1990.

———. *Mystical Writings.* New York: Crossroad, 1990 (Spiritual Classics).

Fox, Matthew, ed. *Hildegard of Bingen's Book of Divine Works with Letters and Songs.* Santa Fe, N.M.: Bear and Co, 1987. Translation of *De operatione Dei.*

———. *Illuminations of Hildegard of Bingen.* Santa Fe, N.M.: Bear and Co, 1985.

Powers, John D. *Holy Human: Mystics for Our Time: Conversations with Hildegard of Bingen [et al.].* Mystic, Conn.: Twenty-Third, 1989.

Schipperges, Heinrich. *Hildegard von Bingen: Mystische Texte der Gotteserfahrung.* 1st ed. Kempten: J. Kösel and F. Pustet, n.d.; Olten [etc.]: Walter, 1978 (Sammlung Kösel 86).

Sölle, Dorothee, and Martina Trauschke. *O Grün des Fingers Gottes: Die Meditationen der Hildegard von Bingen.* Wuppertal: P. Hammer, 1989 (Edition Eine neue Erde 5).

Uhlein, Gabriele. *Meditations with Hildegard of Bingen.* Santa Fe, N.M.: Bear and Co, 1983 (New Age Mystics). English versions compiled from German editions of Hildegard's *Liber vitae meritorum, De operatione Dei, Briefwechsel,* and *Lieder.*

Windstosser, Maria. *Frauenmystik im Mittelalter.* 4.–5. tausend. Kalamazoo, Mich.: Cistercian Publications, 1991.

SELECTIONS (IN ANTHOLOGIES)

"Benedictine Visionaries of the Rhineland: Hildegard of Bingen; Elisabeth of Schönau." In Marcelle Thiébaux, trans., *The Writings of Medieval Women,* pp. 105–34.

"A Benedictine Visionary in the Rhineland: Hildegard of Bingen." In Marcelle Thiébaux, trans., *The Writings of Medieval Women,* 2d ed., pp. 315–48.

Cunningham, Robert. trans. "From *The Book of Divine Works.*" In Karen J. Campbell, ed., *German Mystical Writings,* 3–31.

Dronke, Peter. "Sequence 'Columba aspexit.' " In *Medieval Latin and the Rise of European Love-Lyric.* 2d ed. Oxford: Clarendon, 1968, pp. 75–77 (trans.); pp. 233–35 (Latin with music).

"Excerpts from Hildegard's Works [Letters, *Scivias*]." In Emilie Zum Brunn and Georgette Epiney-Burgard, eds., *Women Mystics in Medieval Europe*, pp. 19–36.

Grant, Barbara L., trans. "Liturgical Songs." In Elizabeth Petroff, ed., *Medieval Women's Visionary Literature*, pp. 157–58.

Kraft, Kent, trans. "The German Visionary: Hildegard of Bingen." In Katharina M. Wilson, ed., *Medieval Women Writers*, pp. 109–30.

Newman, Barbara, trans. "Antiphon for Divine Wisdom," p. 67; "Antiphon for the Holy Spirit," p. 68; "Antiphon for the Angels," p. 69; "Song to the Creator," p. 70; "Alleluia Verse for the Virgin," p. 71. In Jane Hirshfield, ed., *Women in Praise of the Sacred*.

Steele, Francisca, trans. "Hildegard of Bingen, *The Visions of St. Hildegard*." In Amy G. Oden, ed., *In Her Words: Women's Writings in the History of Christian Thought*, pp. 107–13.

———. "The Visions of St. Hildegarde: Extracts from the *Scivias*." In Elizabeth Petroff, ed., *Medieval Women's Visionary Literature*, pp. 151–57.

Scivias (1141–51)

ENGLISH

Hart, Columba, and Jane Bishop, trans. *Scivias*. New York: Paulist Press, 1990 (Classics of Western Spirituality). Introduction by Barbara Newman.

Hozeski, Bruce. *Scivias*. Santa Fe, N.M.: Bear and Co., 1986.

CRITICAL EDITION

Führkötter, Adelgundis, and Angela Carlevaris. *Hildegardis Scivias*. Turnhout: Brepols, 1978 (Corpus christianorum: Continuatio mediaevalis 43–43A). Introduction in German.

GERMAN

Storch, Walburga. *Scivias: Wisse die Wege: Eine Schau von Gott und Mensch in Schöpfung und Zeit*. Augsburg: Pattloch, 1991.

Böckeler, Maura, Sister, ed. and trans. *Wisse die Wege Scivias. Nach dem Originaltext des illuminierten Rupertsberger Kodex*. Salzburg: O. Müller, 1954. The facsimiles reproduce the thirty-five illustrated pages of the original MS (235 l.) of the Codex illuminatus (Hs 1), which disappeared from the Naussauische Landesbibliothek in Wiesbaden in 1945.

Wisse die Wege; Scivias. Berlin: Sankt Augustinus, 1928.

FRENCH

Renard, Jacques, trans. *Scivias: Ou, les trois livres des visions et révélations de l'Edit. Princeps Henri Étienne, 1513.* Paris: R. Chamonal, 1909.

Physica

Patrologia latina v. 197, cols. 1117–352.
Schipperges, Heinrich. *Sudhoffs Archiv* 40 (1956) pp. 41–77.
Riethe, Peter, trans. *Naturkunde; das Buch von dem inneren Wesen der verschiedenen Naturen in der Schöpfung.* Salzburg: Müller, 1959. Translation of *Liber subtilitatum diversarum naturarum creaturarum.*

Causae et curae

CRITICAL EDITION

Kaiser, Paul. *Hildegardis Causae et curae.* Leipzig: Teubner, 1903 (Bibliotheca scriptorum graecorum et romanorum teubneriana).

GERMAN

Breindl, Ellen. *Das grosse Gesundheitsbuch der Hl. Hildegard von Bingen: Leben und Wirken einer bedeutenden Frau des Glaubens: Ratschläge und Rezepte für ein gesundes Leben.* Aschaffenburg: Pattloch, 1983.
Schultz, Hugo. *Ursachen und Behandlung der Krankheiten (Causae et curae).* 4th ed. Heidelberg: Haug, 1983; 1st ed., Munich: Gmelin, 1933.
Schipperges, Heinrich, ed. *Heilkunde; das Buch von dem Grund und Wesen und der Heilung der Krankheiten.* Salzburg: Müller, 1957.
Huber, Alfons, trans. *Der Aebtissin St. Hildegardis myst. Tier- u. Artzneyen-Buch das ist das Buch von den Tieren die auf der Erde umherlaufen dem Gewürm den Vögeln in der Luft und ihren Heilkräften gegen allerlei menschliche Krankheit.* Vienna: Gloriette-Verlag, [192–].

Symphonia harmoniae celestium revelationum

CRITICAL EDITION

Newman, Barbara, ed. *Symphonia: A Critical Edition of the Symphonia armonie celestium revelationum* (Symphony of the harmony of celestial revelations). Ithaca, N.Y.: Cornell University Press, 1988. English and Latin.

LATIN AND GERMAN

Barth, Pudentiana, Mary Immaculata Ritscher, and Joseph Schmidt-Goerg. *Lieder.* Salzburg: Müller, 1969. Antiphons, responses, sequences, and so on, and a morality play, *Ordo virtutum,* in plainsong notation. Latin words, German translation, pp. 214–315.

FRENCH

Bouré, M. A. *Cantique d'après Ste. Hildegarde vierge de l'ordre de S. Benoît: Chant premier.* Worcester: Stanbrook Abbey, 1922.

Liber vitae meritorum

Hozeski, Bruce W., trans. *The Book of the Rewards of life (Liber vitae meritorum).* New York: Garland, 1993 (Garland Library of Medieval literature 89B).

GERMAN

Schipperges, Heinrich. *Der Mensch in der Verantwortung: Das Buch der Lebensverdienste (Liber vitae meritorum).* Salzburg: Müller, 1972.

Liber divinorum operum = De operatione Dei

Gorceix, Bernard. *Le livre des ouvres divines: Visions.* Paris: Albin Michel, 1982 (Spiritualités vivantes, série "Christianisme").
Schipperges, Heinrich, ed. *Gott ist am Werk: Aus dem Buch "De operatione Dei."* Olten: Walter-Verlag, 1958.

Epistolae

ENGLISH

Baird, Joseph L., and Radd K. Ehrman, trans. *The Letters of Hildegard of Bingen.* New York: Oxford University Press, 1994–.

CRITICAL EDITION

Acker, L. van. *Corresponde et epistolarium.* Turnhout: Brepols, 1991 (Corpus christianorum continuatio mediaevalis 91–91A). Text in Latin, introductory matter in German.

GERMAN

Führkötter, Adelgundis, ed. *Briefwechsel [von] Hildegard von Bingen Nach den ältesten Handschriften übers. and nach den Quellen erläutert von Adelgundis Führkötter.* Salzburg: Müller, [1965].

"Hildegard von Bingen [Briefe]." In Wilhelm Oehl, ed., *Deutsche Mystikerbriefe des Mittelalters,* 55–112.

Elisabeth of Schönau (1129–64)

Elisabeth entered the double Benedictine monastery at Schönau at the age of twelve and lived there until her death. She was superior of the nun's convent from 1157. After a serious illness when she was twenty-three, Elisabeth began to experience visions. Her brother, Eckbert, who was the abbot, commanded her to write detailed accounts, which he published. Three books of *Visiones* and the *Liber viarum Dei* survive. Like Hildegard of Bingen, her cousin, Elisabeth's visions denounced heretics and abuses in the church.

SECONDARY WORK

Clark, Anne L. *Elisabeth of Schönau: A Twelfth-Century Visionary.* Philadelphia: University of Pennsylvania Press, 1992 (The Middle Ages series).

CRITICAL EDITIONS

Roth, F. Wilhelm Emil, ed. *Die Visionen der hl. Elisabeth und die Schriften der Aebte Ekbert und Emecho von Schönau.* Brünn: Verlag der "Studien aus dem Benedictiner- und Cistercienser-Orden," 1884. German and Latin.

———. *Das Gebetbuch der hl. Elisabeth von Schönau.* Augsburg, 1886.

Eckbert, *Sanctae Elisabeth vita*. Vol. 195 of *Patrologia latina*. Paris: J.-P. Migne, 1855, cols. 119–94.

SELECTIONS

"Benedictine Visionaries of the Rhineland: Hildegard of Bingen; Elisabeth of Schönau." In Marcelle Thiébaux, trans., *The Writings of Medieval Women*, pp. 134–63.

"Handmaid of God." In Marcelle Thiébaux, trans., *The Writings of Medieval Women*, 2d ed., pp. 349–84.

Oehl, Wilhelm, ed. "Elisabeth von Schönau [Briefe]." In Wilhelm Oehl, ed., *Deutsche Mystikerbriefe des Mittelalters*, pp. 113–39.

Pandiri, Thalia A., trans. "Visions — Book Two." In Elizabeth Petroff, ed., *Medieval Women's Visionary Literature*, pp. 159–70.

Windstosser, Maria. *Frauenmystik im Mittelalter.* Kalamazoo, Mich.: Cistercian Publications, 1991.

Marie de France (mid-twelfth century)

Marie de France is known only through her writings. It is likely that she was born in Normandy in an aristocratic family. She probably spent some time at the English court, and there have been conjectures that she was a sister of King Henry II of England. Her *Lais* were very popular in the Middle Ages. These were stories told in verse, usually dealing with different types of love. She also translated *Aesop's Fables* and wrote other works.

Lais

ENGLISH

Burgess, Glyn S. *The Lais of Marie de France: Text and Context.* Athens: University of Georgia Press, 1987.

Burgess, Glyn S., and Keith Busby, trans. *The Lais of Marie de France.* Harmondsworth, Eng.: Penguin Books, 1986 (Penguin Classics). Translated from the Old French.

Betham, Mary Matilda. *The Lay of Marie and Vignettes in Verse.* New York: Garland, 1978. Includes abstracts of the twelve lays of Marie. Reprint of the 1816 and 1818 eds. published by R. Hunter, London.

Hanning, Robert W., and Joan M. Ferrante, trans. *The Lais of Marie de France: Translated, with an Introduction and Notes, by Robert Hanning and Joan Ferrante; Foreword by John Fowles*. 1st ed. New York: Dutton, 1978.

Mason, Eugene. *French Medieval Romances from the Lays of Marie de France*. New York: AMS Press, 1976; reprint of the 1924 ed. published by Dutton, New York.

Rumble, Thomas C., and Thomas Chestre. *The Breton Lays in Middle English*. Detroit: Wayne State University Press, 1967.

Mason, Eugene. *Lays of Marie de France and Other French Legends*. London: Dent; New York: Dutton, 1966. "First published in this edition 1911" under title *French medieval romances from the lays of Marie de France*.

Lays of Marie de France: And Other French Legends. London: Dent; New York: Dutton, 1911.

Luquiens, Frederick Bliss, trans. *Three Lays of Marie de France*. New York: Holt, 1911.

Rickert, Edith. *Marie de France: Seven of Her Lays Done into English*. London: D. Nutt, 1901.

O'Shaughnessy, Arthur William Edgar. *Lays of France (Founded on the Lays of Marie)*. London: Ellis and Green, 1872.

SELECTIONS

Ferrante, Joan M., trans. "The French Courtly Poet: Marie de France." In Katharina M. Wilson, ed., *Medieval Women Writers*, pp. 64–89.

"A Lai of Courtly Romance and Two Fables: Marie de France." In Marcelle Thiébaux, trans., *The Writings of Medieval Women*, pp. 197–206.

"Marie Is My Name: I Am of France: Marie de France." In Marcelle Thiébaux, trans., *The Writings of Medieval Women*, 2d ed., pp. 277–92.

CRITICAL EDITION

Rychner, Jean, ed. *Le lai de Lanval*. Geneva: Droz, 1958 (Textes littéraires français 77).

FRENCH

Jonin, Pierre, trans. *Les lais de Marie de France: Traduit de l'ancien français*. Paris: H. Champion, 1982 (Traductions des classiques français du moyen âge 13).

Rychner, Jean, ed. *Les lais de Marie de France*. Paris: H. Champion, 1973 (Les classiques français du moyen age 93).

Williams, Harry Franklin, ed. *Les lais de Marie de France*. Englewood Cliffs, N.J.: Prentice-Hall, 1970.

Lods, Jeanne. *Les lais de Marie de France*. Paris: H. Champion, 1959.

Ewert, Alfred, ed. *Lais*. Oxford: Blackwell, 1947.

Williams, Edwin Bucher, ed. *Aucassin et Nicolette and Four Lais of Marie de France*. New York: F. S. Crofts, 1933.

Wattie, Margaret, ed. *The Middle English Lai le freine*. Northampton, Mass., 1929 (Smith College Studies in Modern Languages 10/3).

Tuffrau, Paul. *Les lais de Marie de France*. Paris: L'Édition d'art, 1925 (Epopées et légendes).

Lebesgue, Philéas. *Six lais d'amour*. Paris: E. Sansot, 1913.

OLD NORSE

Cook, Robert, and Mattias Tveitane, eds. *Strengleikar: An old Norse Translation of Twenty-one Old French Lais*. Oslo: Norsk Historisk Kjeldeskrift-institutt, 1979. Old Norse and English.

Rytter, Henrik, trans., and Kjell Venås, eds. *Strengleikar: Eller songbok*. Oslo: Det Norske Samlaget, 1962 (Norrøne bokverk 38).

Guðmundsson, Gutmundur. *Strengleikar*. Rekyavík: Ísafoldarprentsmiðja, 1903.

Keyser, Rudolph, and Carl R. Unger, eds. *Strengleikar eða lioðabok: En samling af romantiske fortaellinger efter bretoniske folkesang (lais)*... Christiana, 1850.

GERMAN AND OLD FRENCH

Rieger, Dietmar. *Die Lais*. Munich: W. Fink, 1980 (Klassische Texte des romanischen Mittelalters in zweisprachigen Ausgaben 19). Introduction in German, text in Old French and German.

Warnke, Karl, ed. *Vier lais der Marie de France, nach der handschrift des Mus. brit. Harl. 978 mit einleitung und glossar*. Halle: Niemeyer, 1925 (Sammlung romanischer übungstexte 2); reprint, Geneva: Slatkine Reprints, 1974.

SPANISH

Valero de Holzbacher, Ana María. *Los lais de María de Francia.* Madrid: Espasa-Calpe, 1978 (Selecciones Austral 47: Narrativa).

ITALIAN AND OLD FRENCH

Neri, Ferdinando, trans. *I lai di Maria di Francia.* Torino: Chiantore, 1946. Old French and Italian on opposite pages.

Guingamor

Weingartner, Russell. *Graelent and Guingamor: Two Breton Lays.* New York: Garland, 1985 (Garland Library of Medieval Literature 37). Anonymous lais, which sometimes have been attributed to Marie de France.

Richthofen, Erich Freiherr von., ed. *Vier altfranzösische Lais (Chievrefeuil, Austic, Bisclavret, Guingamor.* 2d ed. Tübingen: Niemeyer, 1960 (Sammlung romanischer übungstexte 39).

Harris, Julian Earle, ed. "The Lays Gugemar, Lanval and a fragment of Yonec with a Study of the Life and Work of the Author." Ph.D. diss., Columbia University, 1930.

Lommatzsch, Erhard, ed. *Le lai de Guingamor, Le lai de Tydorel (12. jahrhundert).* Berlin: Weidmann, 1922 (Romanische texte 6).

Guingamor, Lanval, Tyolet, Bisclaveret. London: D. Nutt, 1900 (Arthurian Romances Unrepresented in Malory's "Morte d'Arthur" no. 1/2).

Weston, Jessie Laidlay, trans. *Guingamor, Lanval, Tyolet, le Bisclaveret.* New York: AMS Press, [1970]. Reprint of the 1900 ed.

Fables

ENGLISH

Martin, Mary Lou, trans. *The Fables of Marie de France: An English Tradition.* Birmingham, Ala: Summa, 1984. English and French.

Beer, Jeanette M. A., and Jason Carter. *Medieval Fables.* New York: Dodd, Mead, 1983. Selected and translated from British Library, MS Harleian 978.

Ewert, Alfred, and Ronald Carlyle Johnston, eds. *Fables.* Oxford: Blackwell, 1942.

FRENCH

Roquefort, Jean Baptiste Bonaventure de, ed. *Poésies de Marie de France, poéte Anglo-Normand du XIIIe siècle; ou Recueil de lais, fables et autres productions de cette femme célèbre...* Paris: Chez Chasseriau, Libraire, 1820.

GERMAN

Mall, Eduard and Warnke, Karl. *Die fabeln der Marie de France.* Geneva: Slatkine Reprints, 1974. Halle: M. Niemeyer, 1898.

Gumbrecht, Hans Ulrich. *Äsop.* Munich: Fink, 1973. Old French and German.

Warnke, Karl. *Aus dem Esope der Marie de France: Eine Auswahl von dreissig Stücken.* 2d ed. Tübingen: Niemeyer, 1962 (Sammlung Romanischer Übungstexte 9).

Évangile aux femmes

Warnke, Karl, ed. *Das Buch vom Espurgatoire S. Patrice der Marie de France und seine quelle.* Halle: Niemeyer, 1938 (Bibliotheca normannica; Denkmäler normannischer Literatur und Sprache 9). Latin text (two versions in parallel columns) of the *Tractatus de Purgatorio sancti Patricii* of Henry of Saltrey and French translation on opposite pages.

The Évangile aux femmes, an Old-French Satire on Women. Baltimore: Friedenwald, 1895.

Constans, Leopold Eugène. *Marie de Compiègne d'après l'Évangile aux femmes...* Paris: A. Franck, 1876. Text in Old French with modern French translation; commentary and notes in modern French.

Chapter 6

New Spirituality of the Late Twelfth and Thirteenth Centuries

Franciscans

Clare of Assisi (1194–1253)

Clare founded the Poor Clares, the Second (i.e., women's) Order of the Franciscans. The teaching and life of her friend Saint Francis inspired her to give up all her possessions and family wealth and join him in 1212. The Poor Clares originally practiced absolute poverty in which not only the sisters but also the order owned no property of any kind. The order in general was not allowed to continue this practice, but the house in which Clare lived was allowed to continue this as a special privilege. Some of Clare's letters exist, and careful scholarship can discern her own words or work behind the early hagiography of Thomas de Celano and the rule of the Poor Clares.

ENGLISH

Armstrong, Regis J., trans. *Clare of Assisi: Early Documents.* New York: Paulist Press, 1988.

Mary Francis, Mother, trans. *Rule and Testament of St. Clare: Constitutions for Poor Clare Nuns.* Chicago, Ill.: Franciscan Herald Press, 1987.

Armstrong, Regis J., and Ignatius C. Brady, trans. and eds. *Francis and Clare: The Complete Works.* New York: Paulist Press, 1982 (Classics of Western Spirituality).

The Legend and Writings of Saint Clare of Assisi: Introduction, Translation, Studies. St. Bonaventure, N.Y.: Franciscan Institute, 1953. Legend ascribed to Thomas of Celano.

Vyskôcil, Jan Kapistrán, and Vitus Buresh. *The Legend of Blessed Agnes of Bohemia and the Four Letters of St. Clare.* Prague: Universum in Prague, 1932, pp. 136–203. "English translation of the Milan manuscript text of the legend and letters."

Balfour, Charlotte Cornish, et al., trans. *The Life and Legend of the Lady Saint Clare.* London and New York: Longmans, Green and Co., 1910.

Robinson, Raschal, trans. *The Life of Saint Clare Ascribed to Fr. Thomas of Celano of the Order of Friars Minor (A.D. 1255–1261).* Philadelphia: Dolphin Press, 1910.

SELECTIONS

Armstrong, Regis J., and Ignatius C. Brady, trans. "Clare of Assisi." In Serinity Young, ed., *An Anthology of Sacred Texts by and about Women,* p. 66.

————"Clare of Assisi, *The Rule of Saint Clare.*" In Amy G. Oden, ed., *In Her Words: Women's Writings in the History of Christian Thought,* pp. 127–39.

Brady, Ignatius, trans. "The Testament of St. Clare." In Elizabeth Petroff, ed., *Medieval Women's Visionary Literature,* pp. 242–45.

CRITICAL EDITION (LATIN AND FRENCH)

Becker, Marie France, Jean François Godet, and Thaddée Matura. *Écrits.* Paris: Cerf, 1985 (Sources chrétiennes 325). Latin text and French translation on opposite pages.

ITALIAN

Scritti. Vicenza: Edizioni LIEF, 1986. In pocket: facsimile of "Bolla di approvazione della regola, 9 agosto 1253."

Fonti Francescane. Padova Assisi: Edizioni Messaggero Movimento Francescano, 1980, 1987.

Boccali, Giovanni M., and Luciano Canonici. *Opuscula S. Francisci et scripta S. Clarae Assisiensium.* Assisi: Porziuncola, 1978 (Pubblicazioni della Biblioteca storico-francescana dell'Umbria 1). Parallel texts in Latin and Italian; introduction and commentary in Italian.

Boccali, Giovanni M. *Concordantiae verbales opusculorum S. Francisci et S. Clarae Assisiensium.* S. Mariae Angelorum/Assisi: Portiunculae, 1976.

Fortini, Arnaldo, ed. *La leggenda di Santa Chiara d'Assisi.* Rome: Signorelli, 1953.

Battelli, Guido, ed. *La leggenda di Santa Chiara d'Assisi.* Milan: Vita e Pensiero, 1952 (Collana Francescana 12).

Pennacchi, Francesco, ed. *Legenda Sanctae Clarae virginis tratta dal ms. 338 della bibl. comunale di Assisi.* Assisi: Metastasio, 1910.

FRENCH

Vorreux, Damien. *Sainte Claire d'Assise: Documents, biographie, écrits, procès et bulle de canonisation, textes de chroniqueurs, textes législatifs et tables.* Paris: Franciscaines, 1983.

SPANISH

Omaechevarría, Ignacio. *Escritos de Santa Clara y documentos complementarios.* 2d ed. Madrid: Editorial Católica, 1982 (Biblioteca de autores cristianos 314). Latin and Spanish.

Garrido, Javier. *Los escritos de Francisco y Clara de Asis.* 2d ed. Aranzazu: Aldecoa, 1980.

GERMAN

Grau, Engelbert. *Leben und Schriften der Heiligen Klara: Einf., Übers., Anm.* 4th ed. Werl: Dietrich-Coelde-Verlag, 1976 (Franziskanische Quellenschriften 2). 1st and 2d eds. published under title *Leben und Schriften der heiligen Klara von Assisi.*

Agnes of Bohemia (c. 1205–c. 1282)

Brady, Ignatius, trans. "Letter to St. Clare." In Elizabeth Petroff, ed., *Medieval Women's Visionary Literature*, pp. 245–46.

Vyskôcil, Jan Kapistrán. *Legenda Blahoslavené Aneəky a čtyři listy sv. Kláry: překlad středověkého əivotopisu blahoslavené Aneəky dle nejstar šího latinského rukopisu milánského ze začátku XIV. století.* Prague: Nakl. "Universum," 1934.

Vyskôcil, Jan Kapistran and Buresh, Vitus, trans. *The Legend of Blessed Agnes of Bohemia and the Four Letters of St. Clare.* Microfilm —

University of Michigan. "English translation of the Milan manuscript text of the legend and letters," pp. 136–203.

Angela of Foligno (1248–1309)

Angela was a married woman from a wealthy background. Upon her husband's death, she took up a life of prayer and austerity. She became a Third Order Franciscan (i.e., a noncloistered lay affiliate of the order). Angela received frequent visions, the accounts of which were written down in Latin by her confessor. The spirit of early Franciscan piety permeates these visions.

ENGLISH

LaChance, Paul. *Complete Works/Angela of Foligno*. New York: Paulist Press, 1993 (Classics of Western Spirituality).

Steegmann, Mary G., and Algar Labouchere Thorold, trans. *The Book of Divine Consolation of the Blessed Angela of Foligno*. London: Chatto and Windus; New York: Duffield, 1909 (New Medieval Library).

Cruikshank, A. P. L., ed. and trans. *The Book of the Visions and Instructions of Blessed Angela of Foligno*. New York, 1903.

SELECTIONS

Petroff, Elizabeth, trans. "From the *Liber de vere fidelium experientia* (The book of the experience of the truly faithful)." In Elizabeth Petroff, ed., *Medieval Women's Visionary Literature*, pp. 254–63.

Steegmann, Mary G., trans. "Angela de Foligno, *The Book of Divine Consolation*." In Amy G. Oden, ed., *In Her Words: Women's Writings in the History of Christian Thought*, pp. 148–57.

CRITICAL EDITIONS

Thier, Ludger, and Abele Calufetti. *Il libro della Beata Angela da Foligno: Edizione critica*. 2d ed. Rome: Collegii S. Bonaventurae ad Claras Quas, 1985 (Spicilegium Bonaventurianum 25). Text in Italian and Latin; notes in Italian.

Aliquó, Salvatore, ed. *L'esperienza di Dio amore: Il libro*. Rome: Città Nuova, 1972.

Faloci Pulignani, Michele. *Le livre de la bienheureuse Angèle de Foligno: Documents édités par la père Paul Dancoeur; avec le concours de mgr Faloci Pulignani: Texte latin.* Paris: Art Catholique Éditions de la Revue d'ascétique et de mystique, 1925. Text in Latin; introduction and notes in French.

FRENCH

Hello, Ernest. *Le livre des visions et instructions.* Paris: Du Seuil, 1991 (Points: Sagesses Sa39).

Ferré, M. J. *Le livre de l'expérience des vrais fidèles.* Paris: E. Droz, 1927 (Collection de textes franciscains). Text in French and Latin.

Doncoeur, Paul. *Le livre de la bienheureuse soeur Angèle de Foligno: Documents originaux.* Paris: Librairie de l'Art Catholique, 1926. French.

Umiltà of Faenza (1226–1310) (Saint Humilitas)

Umiltà (Humility) is the name Rosana took when she became a nun. She was from a wealthy and high-ranking family of Faenza. She was always pious and intended to live a celibate life, but it became necessary for her to marry when her father died. Her two children died as infants, and after her husband experienced a serious illness, Rosana persuaded her husband to allow her to enter the religious life while he became a lay brother. She was first a nun with the Poor Clares and then a recluse for twelve years. The abbot of the Vallombrosan order persuaded her to found the first convent for women of that order known as Santa Maria Novella alla Malta. In her later years, she also founded a second house. Umiltà was known for preaching by dictating sermons in Latin, miraculously given her by God, since she was said never to have studied Latin. Many older sources do not mention her sermons or do not give credence to Umiltà's authorship. However, it is equally possible that her lack of knowledge of Latin is an exaggeration.

ENGLISH (SELECTIONS)

Pioli, Richard J., trans. "Sermons." In Elizabeth Petroff, ed., *Medieval Women's Visionary Literature,* pp. 247–53.

LATIN

Sala, T. *Sanctae Humilitatis de Faventia: Sermones*. Florence, 1884.

ITALIAN

Zama, Piero. *Santa Umiltà: La Vita e i Sermones*. 2d ed. Faenza: Fratelli
    Lega Editori, 1974 (Memorie di Romagna) pp. 97–173. Partial
    Italian translation of *Sermones*.

Convent at Helfta

The convent at Helfta, near Eisleben in Saxony, is the most
outstanding example in the Middle Ages of a monastic community fostering the intellectual and spiritual life of women. It
was founded in 1228 and moved to Helfta in 1258. It became
an important center of mysticism while Gertrude of Hackeborn
was abbess (1251–92). There has been confusion because this
Gertrude did not write anything that survives, but one of her
younger nuns, known as Gertrude the Great, wrote several of
the most important works of German mysticism. Under Gertrude
of Hackeborn, the convent prospered and developed an excellent scriptorium, choir, and liturgical life. The community was in
sympathy with the Cistercian reforms of Benedictine monasticism
and followed the Cistercian constitutions but never was subject to
the governance of the Cistercian order. After 1271, the Dominican order became very influential at Helfta because the confessors
and spiritual directors for the convent were drawn from the Dominicans from that point. The three authors from Helfta whose
work survives illustrate the way in which Helfta nurtured and
influenced spiritual and intellectual life across a broad range of
women. Mechthild of Hackeborn was probably the sister of the
abbess. She was the choir director and novice mistress. Gertrude
the Great entered the convent at the age of five. Since she reports a dramatic conversion at the age of twenty-five, it is unlikely
that she was in the convent as a religious prodigy like Hildegard of Bingen. The convent at Helfta took in orphans as well as
young girls for schooling. Gertrude was probably in one of those

categories. Mechthild of Magdeburg lived a long time as a Beguine in Magdeburg. It is not certain why she chose to leave her beguinage in Magdeburg and enter Helfta, but by the 1270s, pressure was beginning to mount for the Beguines either to become affiliated with approved religious orders or to disband. Helfta was a refuge and a training ground for women to be scholars, mystics, or craftswomen skilled at making books and other objects.

FOR A RECENT SCHOLARLY ACCOUNT OF THE CONVENT AT HELFTA

Finegan, Mary Jeremy. *The Women of Helfta: Scholars and Mystics.* Athens: University of Georgia Press, 1991.

Gertrude the Great (1256–c. 1302)

Gertrude was an intellectual who grew up at the convent of Helfta. She was much more dedicated to the life of the mind than to that of the spirit until a conversion experience at the age of twenty-five. Gertrude received visions that she later wrote down in Latin in a style that is widely appreciated for its lyricism and beauty. She was an early advocate of the devotion to the Sacred Heart and her life, revelations, and writings revolve around the liturgical rhythm of the monastic community. She worked very closely with Mechthild of Hackeborn, and their works are interwoven to the point that Gertrude's hand was probably involved in the production of Mechthild's work, *Liber spiritualis gratiae.* Gertrude lived virtually her entire life at the monastery. She is sometimes confused with Gertrude of Hackeborn (1251–92), the abbess. Her own duties were not administrative but more likely involved working in the scriptorium and providing music in the liturgy.

WORKS (LATIN AND FRENCH — CRITICAL EDITION)

Hourlier, Jacques, Pierre Doyère, and Jean Marie Clément, eds. *Œuvres spirituelles.* Paris: Cerf, 1967 (Sources chrétiennes 127, 139, 143, 255, 331; Série des textes monastiques d'Occident 19, 25, 27, 48). Latin text and French translation of *Exercitia spiritualia* and *Legatus divinae pietatis.*

Legatus divinae pietatis

ENGLISH

Winkworth, Margaret. *The Herald of Divine Love.* New York: Paulist Press, 1992 (Classics of Western Spirituality).

Barratt, Alexandra. *The Herald of God's Loving Kindness.* Kalamazoo, Mich.: Cistercian Publications, 1991 (The Cistercian Fathers series 35).

The Life and Revelations of Saint Gertrude, Virgin and Abbess, of the Order of St. Benedict. New ed. London: Burns and Oates; New York: Benziger, 1862. Reprint, Westminster, Md.: Newman Press, 1949; Westminster, Md.: Christian Classics, 1983.

SELECTIONS

"Gertrude die Grosse [Briefe]." In Wilhelm Oehl, ed., *Deutsche Mystikerbriefe des Mittelalters,* 240–45.

Love, Peace, and Joy: Devotion to the Sacred Heart of Jesus according to St. Gertrude. Reprint, Rockford, Ill.: TAN Books, 1984.

"The Revelations of St. Gertrude" (Part 2). In Elizabeth Petroff, ed., *Medieval Women's Visionary Literature,* pp. 222–30.

GERMAN

Wieland, Otmar, ed. *Ein botte der götlichen miltekeit.* Ottobeuren Augsburg: Bayerische Benediktinerakademie Kommissionsverlag Winfried-Werk, 1973. Text of the abridged Middle High German translation of *Legatus divina e pietatis* (or, *Insinuationes divinae pietatis*) with title: *Ein botte der götlichen miltekeit.*

SPANISH

Ortega, Timoteo P. *Revelaciones de Santa Gertrudis la Magna, virgen de la Orden de San Benito: Traducidas sobre el texto latino publicado en su más pura integridad por los pp. benedictinos de San Pedro de Solesmes.* 2d ed. Buenos Aires: Benedictina, 1947.

Exercitia spiritualia

ENGLISH

Lewis, Gertrud Jaron, and Jack Lewis, trans. *Spiritual Exercises*. Kalamazoo, Mich.: Cistercian Publications, 1989 (Cistercian Fathers series 49).
Benedictine nun of Regina Laudis, trans. *Exercises*. Westminster, Md.: Newman Press, 1956.

FRENCH

Paradis, Marcelle. *Louange de tendresse: Exercices spirituels inspirés de Sainte Gertrude*. 2d ed. Montreal: Éditions du Héron Bleu, 1983 (Collection souffles et vents).

Mechthild of Hackeborn (1240–98)

Mechthild was the younger sister of Gertrude of Hackeborn, the abbess of Helfta. She entered the convent at the age of seven and eventually became the mistress of novices and teacher of singing. She received visions that were written down. It is likely that they were dictated to Gertrude the Great, a younger nun.

ENGLISH

Halligan, Theresa A. *The Booke of Gostlye Grace of Mechtild of Hackeborn Edited by Theresa A. Halligan*. Toronto: Pontifical Institute of Mediaeval Studies, 1979 (Pontifical Institute of Mediaeval Studies 46). Middle English translation of *Liber spiritualis gratiae*.
Select Revelations of S. Mechtild, Virgin: Taken from the Five Books of Her "Spiritual Grace," and Translated from the Latin by a Secular Priest. London: T. Richardson, 1875 (Medieval Library of Mystical and Ascetical Works).

LATIN

Frederiksen, Britta Olrik. *En Dansk Mechtild-Tradition? En undersøgelse af nogle gammeldanske bønner*. Copenhagen: Akademisk Forlag, 1984 (Universitets- Jubilaets danske Samfunds Skriftserie 493). Text in Danish and Latin; with an English summary.
"Mechtild von Hackeborn [Briefe]." In Wilhelm Oehl, ed., *Deutsche Mystikerbriefe des Mittelalters*, 228–35.

Jöns Anderson Budde, trans., and Robert Geete, ed. *Hel. Mechtilds uppenbarelser (Liber spiritualis gratia).* Stockholm: Norstedt, 1899.

Solesmes, France (Benedictine abbey), ed. *Revelationes Gertrudianae ac Mechtildianae.* Poitiers: H. Oudin, 1875.

Mechthild of Magdeburg (c. 1210–c. 1283)

Mechthild spent most of her life as a Beguine at Magdeburg. Toward the end of her life she moved to the convent at Helfta. This was probably in response to the persecution of the Beguines. She was a mystic and wrote down her visions at the direction of her confessor, a Dominican. Mechthild wrote in a Low German dialect, but her work survives in High German and Latin translations. *The Flowing Light of Godhead,* which was finished at Helfta, had great influence on later mysticism.

Fliessende Licht der Gottheit

Galvani, Christiane Mesch, and Susan L. Clark. *Flowing Light of the Divinity.* New York: Garland, 1991.

Menzies, Lucy. *The Revelations of Mechthild of Magdeburg (1210–1297); or, The Flowing Light of the Godhead.* London: Longmans; New York: Green, [1953].

SELECTIONS

"Brides of the Celestial Bedchamber: Mechthild of Magdeburg; Beatrijs of Nazareth." In Marcelle Thiébaux, trans., *The Writings of Medieval Women,* 2d ed. pp. 385–412.

"Excerpts from Mechthild of Magdeburg's *The Flowing Light of the Godhead.*" In Emilie Zum Brunn and Georgette Epiney-Burgard, eds., *Women Mystics in Medieval Europe,* pp. 54–70.

"[*Flowing Light of the Godhead:* Selections]." In Fiona Bowie, ed., and Oliver Davies, trans., *Beguine Spirituality: Mystical Writings of Mechthild of Magdeburg, Beatrice of Nazareth, and Hadewijch of Brabant,* pp. 49–85.

Hirshfield, Jane, and Davies, Oliver, trans. "Mechthild of Magdeburg." In Jane Hirshfield, ed., *Women in Praise of the Sacred,* pp. 85–96.

Howard, John, trans. "The German Mystic: Mechthild of Magdeburg." In Katharina M. Wilson, ed., *Medieval Women Writers,* pp. 153–85.

"Mechtild von Magdeburg [Briefe]." In Wilhelm Oehl, ed., *Deutsche Mystikerbriefe des Mittelalters,* 222–27.

Menzies, Lucy, trans. *The Flowing Light of the Godhead.* In Elizabeth Petroff, ed., *Medieval Women's Visionary Literature,* pp. 212–21.

————. "From *The Flowing Light of the Godhead.*" In Karen J. Campbell, ed., *German Mystical Writings,* 32–69.

————. "Mechthild of Magdeburg, *The Flowing Light of the Godhead.*" In Amy G. Oden, ed., *In Her Words: Women's Writings in the History of Christian Thought,* pp. 140–47.

"The Soul's Divine Marriage: Mechthild of Magdeburg." In Marcelle Thiébaux, trans., *The Writings of Medieval Women,* pp. 207–19.

Woodruff, Sue. *Meditations with Mechtild of Magdeburg.* Santa Fe, N.M,: Bear and Co., 1982.

CRITICAL EDITION

Neumann, Hans, and Gisela Vollmann-Profe. *Mechthild von Magdeburg, "Das fliessende Licht der Gottheit": Nach der Einsiedler Handschrift in kritischem Vergleich mit gesamten Überlieferung.* Munich: Artemis Verlag, 1990 (Münchener Texte und Untersuchungen zur deutschen Literatur des Mittelalters 100).

GERMAN

Schmidt, Margot, ed., and Hans Urs von Balthasar. *Das fliessende Licht der Gottheit.* Einsiedeln: Benziger, 1956.

Oehl, Wilhelm. *Das fliessende Licht der Gottheit.* Kempten: J. Kösel, 1911; reprinted in 1922.

Simon, Sigmund. *Das fliessende Licht der Gottheit.* Berlin: Oesterheld, 1907.

Preger, Wilhelm. "Dante's Matelda." *Sitzungsberichte* 3 (1873) pp. [185]–240).

Morel, Gall. *Offenbarungen der Schwester Mechthild von Magdeburg, oder, Das fliessende Licht der Gottheit.* Regensburg: G. J. Manz, 1869; reprint, Darmstadt: Wissenschaftliche Buchgesellschaft, 1963, 1980.

Hagiography

The place of hagiography in the study of women's texts has been discussed in the introduction. The late twelfth and thirteenth centuries brought a new popular spirituality focused on radical poverty and sharing in the sufferings of Christ. The Franciscans, Dominicans, and Beguines manifested this spirituality most clearly. In this period, hagiography took on particular importance among women's texts because reflection on lives that illustrated and interpreted these new values became important in a new way. These new values were more concrete and less intellectual than those of the older Benedictine spirituality. Much of the material that we have from the various Beguine communities is hagiography of one sort or another, and the Dominican sisters of the early fourteenth century developed a new genre that recounted the lives of many of their number. The main source for Christian hagiographical works themselves is the *Acta sanctorum,* often abbreviated AA.SS. It is a huge collection, and citations can be confusing. *Acta sanctorum* is arranged in order of the calendar of saints' feasts. Research on a saint should begin by determining her feast day (usually the date of death). For smaller collections like *Butler's Lives of the Saints,* this may be enough. But for *Acta sanctorum,* any information in a citation is essential since there are multiple large volumes for every month, numbering schemes can be obliterated by different bindings, and so on. A more accessible collection of hagiographical sources about women is *Vox benedictina,* which produces translations of a number works of relatively wide interest.

Vox benedictina: A Journal of Translations from Monastic Sources. Saskatoon, Sask.: Peregrina, 1984–.

Analecta bollandiana. Brussels: Société des Bollandistes, 1885–.

Bollandus, Joannes, et al., eds. *Acta sanctorum quotquot toto orbe coluntur . . . antiquis monumentis.* New ed. Paris: Palmé, 1863.

Bertha of Vilich (1056/57)

Holder-Egger, Oswald, ed. "Vita Adelheidis Abbatisae Vilicensis." In *Monumenta germaniae historica: Scriptorum*. Hannover: Hahn, 1888 (Scriptores [supplements 1–12] 15, pt. 2) pp. 754–63.

"Prologus alter ad Vitam S. Adelheidis." *Analecta bollandiana* 2:211–12.

Marsilia (1108)

Marsilia was the abbess of Saint Amand in Rouen in the early twelfth century. She wrote an account of the miracles of Saint Amand, the sixth-century bishop for whom her convent was named.

"Miraculum S. Amandi." *Acta sanctorum*. February 1, pp. 902–3.

Christina of Markyate (c. 1096–c. 1155)

Talbot, Charles H. *The Life of Christina of Markyate: A Twelfth-century Recluse*. 1959; reprint, Oxford: Clarendon; New York: Oxford University Press, 1987 (Oxford Medieval Texts). Latin text with English translation on facing page.

———, trans. "Rejecting Patriarchal Marriage." In Barbara J. MacHaffie, ed., *Readings in Her Story*, pp. 49–53.

———, trans. "Of S. Theodora, a Virgin, Who Is Also Called Christina." In Elizabeth Petroff, ed., *Medieval Women's Visionary Literature*, pp. 144–50.

Clemence of Barking (fl. 1163–69)

Macbain, William, ed. *The Life of St. Catherine*. Oxford: Blackwell, 1964.

Sodergard, O., ed. *La vie d'Edouard le Confesseur*. Uppsala: Almqvist and Wiksell, 1948.

Beguines

The Beguines were a movement of pious women who lived in religious communities without formal vows or many of the other structures of convent life of the Middle Ages. The early Beguines were influenced by the ideal of poverty that was being popularized by Saint Francis of Assisi and Saint Clare. Promotion of radical, literal poverty threatened the established order in the church, so those who advanced such notions were often suspected of heresy. By the end of the thirteenth century the accepted mendicant orders, the Franciscans and Dominicans, were able to press their ideal of poverty only because they also vigorously promoted orthodoxy, including obedience to the authorities of the church in all things. The supporters of the Beguines, in particular Jacques de Vitry, Bishop of Liége, found it necessary to defend the orthodoxy of these women who lived in ways that were not fully approved by the church. The most effective mode of defense was to write accounts of the lives of exemplary women of this movement, illustrating the ways in which they were spiritually inspiring and at the same time emphatically conforming to all the guidelines of the religious life. These hagiographical stories also served to increase the devotion and obedience of the Beguines who would read or hear them from time to time. The surviving *vita* are almost all in Latin or translations based on Latin originals. Most of the Latin *vita* were almost certainly written by men, usually priests. However, in a number of cases, the Latin is a translation or recasting of an account in the vernacular, usually written by Beguines or nuns who knew the subject very closely. The *vita* of Ida of Nivelles, Ida of Leau, Christina Mirabilis, Lutgarde of Aywières, Beatrice of Nazareth, and Julienne de Cornillon fall into this category.

Christina of Saint Trond (Christina Mirabilis)
(1150–1224)

Vita Christinae Mirabilis (Life written by Thomas de Cantimpré with material from Christina's Beguine sisters)

King, Margot, trans. *The Life of Christina Mirabilis*. Toronto: Peregrina, 1989 (Peregrina Translations series 2; Matrologia Latina).
———. *The Life of Christina of Saint Trond*. Saskatoon, Sask.: Peregrina, 1986 (Matrologia Latina Draft Translations series).

SELECTIONS

King, Margot, trans. "The Life of Christina of Saint Trond, Called Christina Mirabilis, by Thomas Cantimpré." In Elizabeth Petroff, ed., *Medieval Women's Visionary Literature*, pp. 185–89.

LATIN

Pinius, J., ed. Thomas de Cantimpré, "Vita beatae Christinae Mirabilis Trudonopoli in Hasbania." *Acta sanctorum* 32 (July 24, v) pp. 637–60.

Marie d'Oignies (1177–1213)

Marie d'Oignies is often credited as the founder of the Beguines, at least in the Low Countries. She was the particular spiritual guide and inspiration of Jacques de Vitry, who became bishop of Liege and then a cardinal and the foremost defender of the Beguines. Thomas of Cantimpré later wrote a supplement to this life.

ENGLISH

King, Margot H. *The Life of Marie d'Oignies.* 2d rev. ed. Toronto: Peregrina, 1989.

SELECTION

King, Margot, trans. "The Life of Marie d'Oignies, by Jacques de Vitry." In Elizabeth Petroff, ed., *Medieval Women's Visionary Literature,* pp. 179–83.

LATIN

Papebroch, D., ed. "Vita Mariae Oigniacensis." *Acta sanctorum* 25 (June 23, v) pp. 542–72.

Supplement by Thomas de Cantimpré

ENGLISH

Thomas de Cantimpré and Hugh Feiss. *Supplement to the Life of Marie d'Oignies.* Saskatoon, Sask.: Peregrina, 1987.

LATIN

Papebroch, D., ed. Thomas de Cantimpré, "Vita Mariae Oigniacensis, supplementum." *Acta sanctorum* 25 (June 23, v) pp. 572–81.

Lutgarde of Aywières (1182–c. 1246)

Lutgarde was renowned for her holiness. She began religious life at the age of twelve in a Benedictine convent and moved to a Cistercian convent at Aywières in 1206. Her holiness was so renowned that the new convent would have elected her abbess even though she did not speak the language used there. She declined the position. Lutgarde was closely associated with the Beguines, and her life was written by Thomas de Cantimpré, using sources from her convent.

ENGLISH

King, Margot H., trans. Thomas de Cantimpré, *The Life of Lutgard of Aywières*. Toronto: Peregrina, 1987 (Peregrina Translations series 9; Matrologia Latina).

LATIN

Henschenius, G., ed. Thomas de Cantimpré, "Vita Lutgardis." *Acta sanctorum* 24 (June 16, iv) pp. 187–210.

Julienne de Cornillon (1193–1258)

Julienne was one of the leaders of the early Belgian beguinages. She was particularly devoted to the adoration of Christ's presence in the sacramental elements of bread and wine. She is credited with being the driving force of the movement that led to the establishment of the feast of Corpus Christi. Her friend Eva may have written her life.

ENGLISH

Newman, Barbara, trans. *The Life of Blessed Juliana of Mont-Cornillon*. Toronto: Peregrina, 1988 (Peregrina Translation series 13 [Matrologia Latina]).

FRENCH

Simenon, G. *Julienne de Cornillon*. Brussels: Editions Universitaires, 1946 (Saints de nos provinces).

LATIN

Henschenius, G., ed. "Vita Julianae Corneliensii." *Acta sanctorum* 10 (April 5, i) pp. 435–75.

Beatrijs van Tienen (Beatrice of Nazareth)
(c. 1200–1268)

Beatrice was from a middle-class family in the town of Tienen, near Louvain, Belgium. She received her early schooling while boarding with a community of Beguines. From the age of ten she lived in Cistercian monasteries for women. She was prioress in a new foundation called Nazareth for the last thirty years of her life. She was talented in the graphic arts as well as writing. She developed a friendship with Ida of Nivelles during the time that she was sent to another Cistercian community to learn to copy manuscripts. Beatrice's *Seven mannieren van Minne* (Seven experiences of love) is a treatise, written in the vernacular, that explains her mystical experiences. The *Life* is based on an autobiography that she wrote, but the text we have was translated and expanded by a chaplain for the monastery. The extent to which this reflects Beatrice's text is a matter for critical discussion.

Life

Ganck, Roger De, trans. *The Life of Beatrice of Nazareth: 1200–1268*. Vol. 1 of *Beatrice of Nazareth*. Kalamazoo, Mich.: Cistercian Publications, 1991 (Cistercian Fathers series 50).

SECONDARY WORKS

Ganck, Roger De. *Beatrice of Nazareth in Her Context*. Vol. 2 of *Beatrice of Nazareth*. Kalamazoo, Mich.: Cistercian Publications, 1991 (Cistercian Studies series 121).

Ganck, Roger De. *Towards Unification with God.* Vol. 3 of *Beatrice of Nazareth.* Kalamazoo, Mich.: Cistercian Publications, 1991 (Cistercian Studies series 122).

ENGLISH AND FLEMISH

Barnouw, Adriaan Jacob, trans. *The Miracle of Beatrice, a Flemish Legend of c. 1300.* New York: Pantheon, 1944. In verse.

CRITICAL EDITION

Reypens, Leonce, ed. *Vita Beatricis; de autobiografie van de Z. Beatrijs van Tienen O. Cist., 1200–1268. In de Latijnse bewerking van de anonieme biechtvader der Abdij van Nazareth te Lier voor het eerst volledig en kritisch uitgegeven.* Antwerp: Ruusbroec-Genootschap, 1964 (Studien en tekstuitgaven van ons geestelijkerf 15). Dutch or Latin.

Seven Experiences of Love

Vekeman, H. W. J., and J. J. Th. M. Tersteeg, eds. *Van seuen manieren van heileger minnen.* Zutphen: Thieme, 1970. At head of title: Beatrijs van Nazareth.
Reypens, Leonce, and Joseph Van Mierlo, eds. *Beatrijs van Nazareth, Seven Manieren van Minne, critisch uitgegeven.* Louvain, 1926.

SELECTIONS

Beatrice of Nazareth. "[*Seven Degrees of Love:* Selections]." In Fiona Bowie, ed., and Oliver Davies, trans., *Beguine Spirituality: Mystical Writings of Mechthild of Magdeburg, Beatrice of Nazareth, and Hadewijch of Brabant,* pp. 86–95.
"Brides of the Celestial Bedchamber: Mechthild of Magdeburg; Beatrijs of Nazareth." In Marcelle Thiébaux, trans., *The Writings of Medieval Women,* 2d ed., pp. 385–412.
Colledge, Eric, trans. "There Are Seven Manners of Loving." In Elizabeth Petroff, ed., *Medieval Women's Visionary Literature,* pp. 200–206.
"Excerpts from Beatrice of Nazareth's 'Vita' and 'The Seven Manners.' " In Emilie Zum Brunn and Georgette Epiney-Burgard, eds., *Women Mystics in Medieval Europe,* pp. 87–94.
Zum Brunn, Emilie, and Georgette Epiney-Burgard, trans. "Beatrice of Nazareth, *The Seven Manners of Love.*" In Amy G. Oden, ed., *In*

Her Words: Women's Writings in the History of Christian Thought,
pp. 121–26.

Christine von Stommeln (1242–1312)

Christine is sometimes known as "Kölnische Christine" because
she came from Cologne. Christine saw visions from very early
in her life onward. She was a Beguine from 1255. She suffered
extraordinary pain, including the stigmata. Her spiritual director
was a Swiss Dominican, Peter Dacus.

"Christine von Stommeln [Letters]." In Wilhelm Oehl, ed., *Deutsche
Mystikerbriefe des Mittelalters,* 246–75.
Papebroch, D., ed. "Vita Christinae Stumbelensis." *Acta sanctorum* 25
(June 22, v) pp. 367–87. "Acta Christinae Stumbelensis." *Acta
sanctorum* 1 (June 22, v) pp. 236–367.

Agnes d'Hourcourt (c. 1274)

Agnes was a lady of honor to Princess Isabella, the sister of
Louis IX. Agnes was a nun and abbess at Longchamp and wrote
the life of Blessed Isabella.

"Vita Elisabethae seu Isabellae." *Acta sanctorum* 40 (August 31, vi)
pp. 798–808.

Philippine de Porcellet (c. 1300)

Philippine was a Beguine and a disciple of Douceline, the founder
of a house of Beguines that was associated with the Franciscans.
Philippine wrote the life of Douceline in Provençal.

Life of Douceline

PROVENÇAL AND FRENCH

Gout, Raoul, ed. and trans. *La vie de Sainte Douceline: Texte provençal
du XIVe siècle.* Paris: Bloud et Gay, 1927.
Albanes, J. H., ed. and trans. *La vie de Sainte Douceline: Fondatrice
des beguines de Marseille, composée au treizième siècle en langue
provençale.* Marseilles: Camoin, 1879.

Anonymous Beguine (thirteenth century)

Verbum Jesu Christi ad Beginam Tungerensem. In Stephanus Axters, ed., "De anonieme Begijn van Tongerenen haar mystieke dialoog." *Ons Geestlijk Erf* 15/1 (1941) pp. 88–97.

Hadewijch (thirteenth century)

Hadewijch lived in the area that is now Belgium during the first half of the thirteenth century. Little is known of her life. It can be inferred from her writings that she was well educated and was probably the head of a Beguine community. She encountered opposition to her leadership and personally faded into obscurity. She wrote poems, letters, and accounts of visions (forty-five strophic poems; sixteen couplet poems; fourteen visions; thirty-one letters). These works, written in Flemish, reflect a life of prayer, good works, and Christian love.

WORKS (ENGLISH)

Hart, Columba, ed. and trans. *Hadewijch, the Complete Works.* New York: Paulist Press, 1980 (Classics of Western Spirituality).

SELECTIONS

Colledge, Eric, trans. "Hadewijch of Brabant, *Letters and Visions.*" In Amy G. Oden, ed., *In Her Words: Women's Writings in the History of Christian Thought,* pp. 114–20.
———. "Letters to a Young Beguine." In Elizabeth Petroff, ed., *Medieval Women's Visionary Literature,* pp. 189–95.
Davies, Oliver, and Columba Hart, trans. "Hadewijch of Antwerp." In Jane Hirshfield, ed., *Women in Praise of the Sacred,* pp. 99–104.
"Excerpts from the Works of Hadewijch I and Hadewijch II." In Emilie Zum Brunn and Georgette Epiney-Burgard, eds., *Women Mystics in Medieval Europe,* pp. 113–39.
Hart, Mother Columba, trans. "Visions." In Elizabeth Petroff, ed., *Medieval Women's Visionary Literature,* pp. 195–200.
Hughes, Sheila, trans. "Hadewijch II." In Jane Hirshfield, ed., *Women in Praise of the Sacred,* pp. 105–9.

Rombauts, Edward, and N. de. Paepe, eds. *Middelnederlandse tekst en moderne bewerking, met een inleiding door E. Rombauts en N. de Paepe.* Zwolle: W. E. J. Tjeenk Willink, 1961.

"[Selections]." In Fiona Bowie, ed., and Oliver Davies, trans., *Beguine Spirituality: Mystical Writings of Mechthild of Magdeburg, Beatrice of Nazareth, and Hadewijch of Brabant,* pp. 96–125.

Vanderauwera, Ria. "The Brabant Mystic: Hadewijch." In Katharina M. Wilson, ed., *Medieval Women Writers,* pp. 186–203.

Visions

FRENCH

P., Fr. J.-B. M., trans. *Visions.* Paris: O.E.I.l., 1987 (Les deux rives).

Vekeman, H. W. J., ed. *Het visioenenboek van Hadewijch: Uitgegeven naar handschrift 941 van de Bibliotheek der Rijksuniversiteit te Gent.* Nijmegen Bruges: Dekker and Van de Vegt Orion, 1980.

Mommaers, Paul. *De Visioenen van Hadewijch.* Nijmegen Bruges: B. Gottmer Emmaus, 1979 (Spiritualiteit 15).

Plassmann, J. O. *Vom Göttlichen Reichtum der Seele: Altflämsiche Frauenmystik: Aus dem Altflämischen übertragen.* Düsseldorf: E. Diederichs, 1951.

Letters

Mierlo, Jozef van. *Brieven.* Antwerp: Standaard-Boekhandel, 1947.

"Hadewijch [Briefe]." In Wilhelm Oehl, ed., *Deutsche Mystikerbriefe des Mittelalters,* 721–33.

Strophic Poems

Plas, Rose Vande, trans. *Amour est tout: Poèmes strophiques.* Paris: Tequi, 1984 (Livre d'or des écrits mystiques). Translation from Middle Dutch.

Ortmanns, M. *Van liefde en minne: De Strofische gedichten hertaald door M. Ortmanns.* Tielt: Lannoo, 1982. Dutch and Middle Dutch.

Paepe, N. de. *Strofische gedichten.* 2d ed. Gent: Story-Scientia, 1972.

Other Poetry

Mengeldichten of rijmbrieven. Bruges: Tabor, 1988.

Paepe, N. de. *Een bloemlezing uit haar werken.* Amsterdam and Brussels: Elsevier, 1979.

Miere herten licht doolt na U al. Hasselt: Heideland-Orbis, 1973.

Vingers van glas: Gedichten. Winschoten: Van der Veen, 1968.

Hadewijch; een bloemlezing uit hare werken. Amsterdam: Elsevier, 1950.

Dominican Chronicles

In the late thirteenth or early fourteenth century, the Dominican nuns in the region where Germany, France, and Switzerland come together began the practice of writing short biographies or obituaries of the sisters who had recently lived among them. These resemble hagiography in the focus on God's action in the life in question rather than on external events. However, these are not intended to make a case for canonization of any individual, nor are they examples of holy people from far away in time or distance. The first of these was assembled by Katharina of Gebsweiler (variously spelled Gebweiler, Gerberschwerber, Gerbersweiler), prioress of the convent of Unterlinden near Colmar in Alsace. This contained lives of about fifty nuns and became the model for a number of other collections listed below and a practice that continues among Dominican sisters today. A specific person can sometimes be credited as the author or compiler of a collection, but these collections are usually anonymous. In any case, these chronicles were composed within the convents by the sisters themselves and are important texts of women's communities of the Middle Ages. While the practice is characteristic of Dominicans, other orders also participated, as shown by the chronicle of the Bickenkloster of Villingen, a community of Poor Clares (Franciscans).

FOR DISCUSSION OF THESE CHRONICLES

Gehring, Hester McNeal Reed. "The Language of Mysticism in South German Dominican Convent Chronicles of the Fourteenth Century." Ph.D. diss., University of Michigan, 1957. Available from University Microfilms International.

Lives of the Sisters at Unterlinden:
Katharina of Gebsweiler (c. 1250–1330/40)

SELECTIONS

"Unterlinden [from the Lives of the Sisters]." In Simon Tugwell, O.P., ed., *Early Dominicans: Selected Writings*. New York: Paulist Press, 1982 (Classics of Western Spirituality) pp. 417–24.

LATIN

Wittmer, Charles. *L'obituaire des Dominicaines d'Unterlinden: Édition critique du manuscrit 576 de la bibliotheque de la ville de Colmar*. Strasbourg: P. H. Heitz, 1946. Text of MS in Latin.

Ancelot-Hustache, Jeanne, ed. "*Vitae sororum* d'Unterlinden: Édition critique du manuscrit 508 de la bibliotheque de Colmar." *Archives d'histoire doctrinale et litteraire du moyen âge*. Paris: J. Vrin, 1930, 5:317–509.

GERMAN

Wilms, Hieronymus. *Das Beten der Mystikerinnen: Dargestellt nach den Chroniken der Dominikanerinnen-Klöster zu Adelhausen, Diessenhofen, Engeltal, Kirchberg, Oetenbach, Töß und Unterlinden*. Leipzig: O. Harrassowitz, 1916.

Oehl, Wilhelm, ed. "Kloster Unterlinden." In Wilhelm Oehl, ed., *Deutsche Mystikerbriefe des Mittelalters*, pp. 197–204.

Kirchberger Schwesternbuch: Elisabeth von Kirchberg
(c. 1296 or early fourteenth century)

TWO TEXTS FROM KIRCHBERG NEAR SULZ IN WÜRTTEMBERG
(1) SIXTY-FOUR LIVES; (2) TWENTY-THREE LIVES

Roth, F. W. E., ed. "Die Nonnen von Kirchberg." *Alemannia* 21 (1893) pp. 103–23.

Birlinger, A., ed. "Die Nonnen von Kirchberg bei Haigerloch." *Alemannia* 11 (1883) pp. 1–20.

Adelhausen Chronicle: Anna von Munzingen (c. 1327)

LIVES OF THIRTY-FOUR SISTERS FROM ADELHAUSEN
NEAR FREIBURG IM BREISGAU

Die Adelhauser Urbare von 1327 und 1423. Freiburg im Breisgau:
Stadtarchiv Freiburg im Breisgau, 1988 (Veröffentlichungen aus
dem Archiv der Stadt Freiburg im Breisgau 18). Registers in Middle
High German and German.

König, J., ed. "Die Chronik der Anna von Munzingen." *Freiburger
Diözesan-Archiv* 13 (1880) pp. 129–236; text pp. 153–93.

Büchlein der Gnaden überlasst (Account of the Nuns at Engeltal): Christina Ebner (d. 1356)

LETTERS

"Christine Ebner [Briefe]." In Wilhelm Oehl, ed., *Deutsche Mystikerbriefe des Mittelalters,* 344–47.

Weinhandl, Margarete, ed. and trans. *Deutsches Nonnenleben: Das
Leben der Schwestern zu Töß und der Nonne von Engeltal Büchlein
von der Gnaden überlast.* Munich: O. C. Recht, 1921 (Katholikon
Werke und Urkunden 2) pp. 263–325.

Schröder, Karl, ed. *Der Nonne von Engelthal Büchlein von der Genaden
überlast.* Tübingen: Litterarischer Verein in Stuttgart, 1871. (Hotch-
kiss: *Bibliothek des litterarischen Vereins* 108 [Tübingen, 1871]
1–69.)

SECONDARY

Voit, Gustav. *Engelthal: Geschichte eines Dominikanerinnenklösters im
Nürnberger Raum.* Nuremberg: Korn and Berg, 1977 (Altnürn-
berger Landschaft; Schriftenreihe 26/26).

Ulmer Schwesternbuch (c. 1330)

Unknown convent in Swabia.

Roth, F. W. E., ed. "Ulmer Schwesternbuch." *Alemannia* 21 (1893)
pp. 123–48.

Lives of the Sisters from Oetenbach (Zurich) (c. 1340)

Zeller-Werdmüller, H., and J. Bächtold, eds. "Die Stiftung des Klosters Oetenbach und das Leben der seligen Schwestern daselbst." *Zürcher Taschenbuch,* n.s., 12 (1889) pp. 213–76.

Collection from Weilen an Neckar (c. 1350)

Anonymous. Lives of twenty-seven nuns from a Dominican convent near Eislingen.

Bihlmeyer, Karl, ed. "Mystisches Leben in dem Dominikanerinnenklöster Weiler bei Eslingen im 13. und 14. Jahrhundert." *Würtembergische Vierteljahreshefte für Landesgeschichte,* n.s., 25 (1916) pp. 61–93.

Katharinental Bei Dießenhofen (Switzerland)

Anonymous. Lives of about fifty nuns from the late fourteenth century.

Birlinger, A., ed. "Die Nonnen von St. Katharinental be Dieszenhofen." *Alemannia* 15 (1887) pp. 150–83.

Chronik des Bickenklosters zu Villingen

Glatz, Karl Jordan, ed. *Chronik des Bickenklosters zu Villingen 1238 bis 1614.* Stuttgart: Litterarischer Verein; Tübingen: L.F. Fues (Bibliothek des literarischen Vereins in Stuttgart 151).
Haider, Ursula. "Ursula Haider [Briefe]." In Wilhelm Oehl, ed., *Deutsche Mystikerbriefe des Mittelalters,* pp. 650–56.

Chronicle of the Lives of the Sisters at Töß
See Elsbeth Stagel

Elsbeth Stagel (d. 1360)

Elsbeth was a Dominican sister at the convent at Töß near Winterthur in the diocese of Constance. In addition to being responsible for writing the chronicle of the convent, she was a disciple and confidant of Henry Suso (Heinrich Seuse), the famous Swiss Dominican mystic. In an interesting reversal of the accustomed pattern, Elsbeth wrote down the things that Henry told her of his life and later presented them to him. While there is some debate about how much of Elsbeth's text survives, she wrote the original foundation of the autobiography of Henry Suso, the *Life of the Servant.*

Chronicle of the Lives of the Sisters at Töß (*Tößer Viten*)

Wilms, Hieronymus. *Das älteste Verzeichnis der deutschen Domini-kanerinnenklöster.* Leipzig, 1928 (Quellen und Forschungen zur Geschichte des Dominikanerordens in Deutschland 24).

Weinhandl, Margarete. *Deutsches Nonnenleben: Das Leben der Schwestern zu Töß und der Nonne von Engeltal Büchlein von der Gnaden überlast.* Munich: O.C. Recht, 1921 (Katholikon Werke und Urkunden 2) pp. 115–260.

Vetter, Ferdinand, and Johannes Meier, eds. *Das leben der schwestern zu Töß.* Berlin: Weidmann, 1906 (Deutsche Texte des Mittelalters 6).

Life of Henry Suso

ENGLISH

Tobin, Frank J. *Henry Suso: The Exemplar, with Two German Sermons.* New York: Paulist Press, 1989 (Classics of Western Spirituality).

Edward, Sister M. Ann, trans. *The Exemplar: Life and Writings of Blessed Henry Suso, O.P.* Dubuque, Iowa: Priory Press, 1962. Translation of: Nikolaus Heller, *Des Mystikers Heinrich Seuse, O. PR., deutsche Schriften.*

The Life of the Servant. Paperback ed. Greenwood, S.C.: Attic Press, 1982 (Classics of Mysticism).

The Life of the Servant. London: James Clarke, 1952. A translation of the Bihlmeyer edition of the author's autobiography: *Das Buch, das da heisset der Seuse.*

Knox, Thomas Francis. *The Life of Blessed Henry Suso.* London: Burns, Lambert, and Oates, 1865.

CRITICAL EDITION

Bihlmeyer, Karl, ed. *Deutsche Schriften.* Frankfurt am Main: Minerva, 1961; reprint of Stuttgart: W. Kohlhammer, 1907 ed.

GERMAN

Das Leben des seligen Heinrich Seuse. Düsseldorf: Patmos, 1966.
Heller, Nikolaus. *Deutsche Schriften.* Regensburg: Manz, 1926.

SELECTIONS

Hofmann, Georg. *Deutsche mystische Schriften.* Düsseldorf: Patmos, 1986; reprint of 1st ed., 1966.
Scholz, Wilhelm von, et al. *Heinrich Suso, eine Auswahl aus seinen deutschen Schriften.* Munich and Leipzig: R. Piper, 1906 (Die Fruchtschale 14).
Zeller, Winfried, et al. *Mystische Schriften.* Munich: E. Diederichs, 1988.

FRENCH

Le Cerf, Nicolas, trans. *Oeuvres spirituelles de Henry Suso, personnage fort celebré en doctrine, and saincteté de vie.* Paris: Chez Guillaume Chaudiere, 1586. In French; includes meditations in Latin.

Margaret Ebner (c. 1291–1351)

Margaret was a Dominican nun in the convent of Saint Mary Medingen. She was well known for her holiness and was much admired by her spiritual director, Henry of Nördlingen. Margaret and Henry met in person only eight times because Henry was exiled for supporting Pope John XXII in his dispute with Louis the Bavarian over the succession to the throne of Bavaria while Margaret was an ardent supporter of Louis. The relationship between nun and confessor took place largely via letters, some of which still exist. Margaret was ill for most of her life. But her suffering was accompanied by emotions of spiritual consolation as well as visions and revelations. Henry of Nördlingen considered her to be a prophet and sought advice from her, something that was unusual for a priest to do unless the nun was considered a saint. At Henry's insistence, Margaret wrote down a description of her visions that is known as *Offenbarungen* or *Revelations*.

ENGLISH

Hindsley, Leonard P., trans. and ed., *Margaret Ebner, Major Works.* New York: Paulist Press, 1993 (Classics of Western Spirituality).

GERMAN

"Margarete Ebner [Briefe]." In Wilhelm Oehl, ed., *Deutsche Mystiker-briefe des Mittelalters,* pp. 333–43.

Windstosser, Maria. *Frauenmystik im Mittelalter.* 4.–5. tausend. Kalamazoo, Mich: Cistercian Publications, 1991.

Prestel, Josef. *Die Offenbarungen der Margaretha Ebner und der Adelheid Langmann.* Weimar: Herman Böhlaus, 1939 (Mystiker des Abendlandes 4) pp. 7–109.

Windstosser, Maria, ed. *Deutsche Mystiker.* Vol. 5 of *Frauenmystik im Mittelalter.* Kempten and Munich: Kösel, 1919.

"Margaretha Ebner an Heinrich von Nördlingen [1346]." In Philipp Strauch, *Margaretha Ebner und Heinrich von Nördlingen: Ein beitrag zur Geschichte der deutschen Mystik.* Freiburg and Tübingen: Mohr, 1882, pp. 281–83; reprint, Amsterdam: Schippers, 1966.

Adelheid Langmann (c. 1305–75)

Adelheid was from Nuremberg and joined the convent at Engelthal with Christine Ebner. She was known for her holiness. Her revelations are not as well regarded as those of many of the other German mystics because they offer a less profound appreciation of suffering and contain more childlike and colorful imagery.

Langmann, Adelheid. "Adelheid Langmann." In Wilhelm Oehl, ed., *Deutsche Mystikerbriefe des Mittelalters,* pp. 393–96.

Prestel, Josef. *Die Offenbarungen der Margaretha Ebner und der Adelheid Langmann.* Weimar: Herman Böhlaus, 1939 (Mystiker des Abendlandes 4) pp. 113–83.

Strauch, Philipp, ed. *Die offenbarungen der Adelheid Langmann, klosterfrau zu Engelthal.* Strasbourg: Trübner, 1878 (Quellen und forschungen zur sprach- und culturgeschichte der germanischen völker 26).

Marguerite d'Oingt (c. 1240–1310)

Marguerite was the prioress of the Carthusian convent of Poletin, near Lyons. She wrote well in Latin and Provençal and composed a life of Saint Beatrice and records of her own visions.

SELECTION

Pioli, Richard J., trans. "The Mirror of St. Marguerite d'Oingt." In Elizabeth Petroff, ed., *Medieval Women's Visionary Literature,* pp. 290–94.

ENGLISH

Blumenfeld-Kosinski, Renate. *The Writings of Margaret of Oingt, Medieval Prioress and Mystic (d. 1310).* Newburyport, Mass.: Focus Information Group, 1990 (Focus Library of Medieval Women).

CRITICAL EDITION

Duraffour, Antonin, Pierre Gardette, and Paulette Durdilly, eds. *Les oeuvres de Marguerite d'Oingt.* Paris: Les Belles lettres, 1965 (Lyons Facultés catholiques Institut de linguistique romane 21). Provençal and French on opposite pages.

Schwester Katrei

In the works of Meister Eckhart (d. 1327), the great Dominican mystic and center of controversy about the nature of mystical union with God, there is often found a tractate called "Schwester Katrei." In this treatise, a mysterious woman appears and enters a dialogue with the confessor in which she teaches him much about ascetic practice and mystical relationship with God. The only information given about the woman is that she is Eckhart's daughter from Strasbourg. The precise meaning of this is not clear. In addition, recent scholarship generally does not accept that it was actually written by Meister Eckhart, although there are a number of ways in which the mysticism of this treatise is very close to Eckhart's. The authorship is thus unknown, but the contents, in particular the discussion of Mary Magdalene among the apostles, is particularly sympathetic to women. Female authorship is thus not unlikely.

ENGLISH

Borgstädt, Elvira, trans. "The 'Sister Catherine' Treatise." In Bernard McGinn, ed., *Meister Eckhart: Teacher and Preacher.* New York: Paulist Press, 1986 (Classics of Western Spirituality) pp. 347–87.

"Sister Katrei." In Franz Pfeiffer, ed., and C. de B. Evans, trans. *Meister Eckhart.* London: John M. Watkins, 1924, pp. 312–34.

GERMAN

Pfeiffer, Franz, ed. *Meister Eckhart.* Leipzig: G. J. Göschen, 1845–57 (Deutsche Mystiker des vierzehnten Jahrhunderts 2) pp. 448–75; reprint, Aalen: Scientia Verlag, 1962.

Chapter 7

Women Accused of Heresy

The women cited in the following section were officially accused of heresy by the church. That is to say, they were professed members of the Christian church who then espoused beliefs that were contrary to the essential faith of that church. Heresy was theological treason. The political aspect of this is not to be underestimated, as can be readily seen in the case of Joan of Arc. Those who were prosecuted as heretics presented a clearly perceived threat to the religious and social order of medieval Europe. Some who were prosecuted and even burned as heretics have been defended by scholars and other observers as being orthodox in matters of faith, others were clearly radical and revolutionary; still others were simple and bewildered folk whose views were pliable and liable to change with their surroundings.

Marguerite Porete (d. 1310)

Marguerite was a Beguine in northern France or Flanders. Little is known of her early life. In 1300, at the city of Valenciennes, her *Mirror of Simple Souls* was condemned as heretical because her teaching about "free souls" challenged the authority of the visible church. Marguerite's views did not change, and she continued her condemnation of abuses in the church. She was condemned as a relapsed heretic and burned in Paris on June 1, 1310. The condemnation of her book hampered its distribution, so that Marguerite has not been published or studied as much as other authors of her caliber.

ENGLISH

Babinsky, Ellen L., trans. *The Mirror of Simple Souls*. New York: Paulist Press, 1993 (Classics of Western Spirituality).

Crawford, Charles. *A Mirror for Simple Souls*. New ed. New York: Crossroad, 1990 (Spiritual Classics). Introduction by Anne L. Barstow.

SELECTIONS

Bryant, Gwendolyn, trans. "The French Heretic Beguine: Marguerite Porete." In Katharina M. Wilson, ed., *Medieval Women Writers*, pp. 204–27.

———. "Marguerite Porete, *The Mirror of Simple Souls*." In Amy G. Oden, ed., *In Her Words: Women's Writings in the History of Christian Thought*, pp. 158–69.

Dronke, Peter. *Women Writers of the Middle Ages*, pp. 217–27 (English); pp. 275–78 (Latin and French).

———, trans. "Beloved, What Do You Want of Me?" In Jane Hirshfield, ed., *Women in Praise of the Sacred*, pp. 97–98.

Levine, Don Eric, trans. "The Mirror of Simple Souls Who Are Annihilated and Who Only Remain in the Will and Desire for Love." In Elizabeth Petroff, ed., *Medieval Women's Visionary Literature*, pp. 294–98.

"Marguerite Porete's 'Approbatio' and Excerpts from 'The Mirror of Simple Souls.'" In Emilie Zum Brunn and Georgette Epiney-Burgard, eds., *Women Mystics in Medieval Europe*, pp. 163–75.

CRITICAL EDITIONS (LATIN WITH FRENCH)

Verdeyen, Paul, and Romana Guarnieri. *Margaretae Porete Speculum simplicium animarum*. Turnhout: Brepols, 1986 (Corpus christianorum continuatio mediaevalis 69). Includes on facing pages the Middle French and Latin versions of the text; introduction in French.

Margareta Porete, Speculum simplicium animarum: Instrumenta lexicologica latina. Turnhout: Brepols, 1986 (Instrumenta lexicologica latina, series A, Enumeratio formarum, con cordantia formarum, index formarum a tergo ordinatarum, fasc. 34). Latin text, preface in French. Four microfiches in pocket.

Doiron, Marilyn. "The 'Mirror of Simple Souls': A Middle English Translation; with an Appendix: The Glosses by 'M.N.' and Richard

Methley to 'The Mirror of Simple Souls,' by Edmund Colledge and Romana Guarnieri." *Archivio italiano per la storia della pietà* 5 (1968) pp. 241–382.

Guarnieri, Romana. "Il 'Miroir des simples ames' di Margherita Porete." *Archivio italiano per la storia della pietà* 4 (1965) pp. 501–635.

GERMAN

Gnädinger, Louise. *Der Spiegel der einfachen Seelen: Wege der Frauen-mystik.* Zurich: Artemis, 1987.

Na Prous Boneta (c. 1290–1325)

Prous Boneta was a visionary who was burned as a heretic in Montpellier in 1325. She had been associated with the Spiritual Franciscans, a group declared heretical for its advocacy of radical "apostolic poverty" for the institutional church. Na Prous (Na is a contraction of "Domina," an honorific title) had come to believe that she was the herald of a new age and an incarnation of the Holy Spirit. The only source for Na Prous Boneta is the Latin transcript of the statement she made to the Inquisition in the Provençal language.

LATIN AND ENGLISH

May, William Harold, trans. "The Confession of Prous Boneta, Heretic and Heresiarch." In J. H. Mundy, R. W. Emery, and B. N. Nelson, eds., *Essays in Medieval Life and Thought.* New York: Columbia University Press, 1955, pp. 3–30.

SELECTION (ENGLISH)

Petroff, Elizabeth, trans. "The Confession of Na Prous Boneta, Heretic and Heresiarch, Carcassone, France, 6 August 1325." In Elizabeth Petroff, ed., *Medieval Women's Visionary Literature,* pp. 284–90.

Testimonies before Inquisitors

Jacques Fournier was a bishop assigned to be an inquisitor during the Albigensian crusade. The transcripts of the testimony given by those convicted of heresy by him were preserved. While the expression of the people was certainly affected by the fact that they were on trial and under duress, the women's testimonies are remarkably fresh and unstereotyped. It is likely that the uneducated women who were being questioned by this inquisitor knew that their best chance for a light punishment was not to try to guess what the inquisitor wanted to hear, but rather to tell what had happened in such a way that the greater part of the blame would fall on someone else.

Aude Faure

Dronke, 213–15 (trans.); 271–73 (text).

Grazida Lizier

Dronke, 204–5 (trans.); 265–69 (text).

Guillemette Bathegan

Dronke, 212 (trans.); 270–71 (text).

Mengarde Buscalh

Dronke, 210 (trans.); 269–70 (text).

Sybille Pierre

Dronke, 211 (trans.).

SOURCES

Dronke, Peter. *Women Writers of the Middle Ages*. Cambridge: Cambridge University Press, 1984.

Duvernoy, Jean. *Le registre d'inquisition de Jacques Fournier, évêque de Pamiers (1318–1325)*. Paris: Mouton, 1977 (Civilisations et sociétés 43).

———. *Le registre d'inquisition de Jacques Fournier, évêque de Pamiers (1318–1325): Manuscrit no Vat. Latin 4030 de la Bibliothèque vaticane.* Toulouse: Privat, 1965. Text in Latin.

Joan of Arc (1412–31)

Joan was the daughter of a peasant. During her early teens she began hearing voices, which she understood to be messages from saints. She prophesied to the king of France what military actions he should take to save France from the English. She wore armor and led the troops into battle at Orleans in 1429. Her fortunes reversed the next year when she was captured by the English in the spring. She was tried on charges of witchcraft and heresy in February of 1431. Joan was convicted, and in some way recanted. However, she soon resumed wearing male clothing, which was a practice she had agreed to abandon in her recantation. She was condemned and burned as a relapsed heretic at the end of May. The trial and its verdict were revised by a court under Pope Callistus III in 1456, and she was canonized a saint in 1920. She is a patron saint of France. Joan did not write anything, but she dictated some letters, and the transcripts of her trials contain substantial verbatim quotations from her.

Trial

ENGLISH

Trial of Joan of Arc. Birmingham, Ala.: Notable Trials Library, 1991. Trial for heresy and sorcery, Feb.–Mar. 1431, at Rouen. "Trial for Relapse [May 28–30, 1431]": pp. 349–66. Introduction to reprint ed. by Alan Dershowitz. Reprint. Originally published: *Trial of Jeanne d'Arc.* 1st ed. New York: Gotham House, 1932.

Jones, A. E. *The Trial of Joan of Arc.* London: Barry Rose Ltd., 1980.

Scott, Walter Sidney, trans. *The Trial of Joan of Arc: Being the Verbatim Report of the Proceedings from the Orleans Manuscript.* London: Folio Society, 1956.

Barrett, Wilfred Phillips, et al., eds. and trans. *The Trial of Jeanne d'Arc: A Complete Translation of the Text of the Original Documents, with an Introduction.* London: Routledge, 1931.

LATIN AND FRENCH

Oursel, Raymond, ed. and trans. *Le procès de condamnation et le procès de réhabilitation de Jeanne d'Arc.* Paris: Denoéel, 1959.

Marchand, Jean, and Guillaume Manchon, eds. *Le procès de condamnation de Jeanne d'Arc: Reproduction en fac-similé du manuscrit authentique, sur vélin, no. 1119 de la Bibliothèque de l'Assemblée nationale.* Paris: Plon, 1955.

Champion, Pierre Honoré Jean Baptiste, et al., eds. and trans. *Procès de condamnation de Jeanne d'Arc: Texte, traduction et notes.* Paris: E. Champion, 1920 (Bibliothèque du XVe siècle 22–23).

O'Reilly, Ernest Marie Jacques Farell, et al., comps. *Les deux procès de condamnation, les enquêtes et la sentence de réhabilitation de Jeanne d'Arc; mis pour la première fois intégralement en français d'après les textes latins originaux officiels.* Paris: Plon, 1868.

Quicherat, Jules. *Procès de condamnation et de réhabilitation de Jeanne d'Arc, dite La Pucelle.* Paris: Renouard, 1841. Latin (chiefly) or French.

FRENCH

Lemaître, Jean, ed. *Instrument public des sentences portées les 24 et 30 mai 1431 par Piérre Cauchon et Jean Le Maître contre Jeanne La Pucelle.* Paris: Librairie d'Argences, 1954 (Documents et recherches relatifs à Jeanne la Pucelle 2).

Brasillach, Robert, ed. *Le procès de Jeanne d'Arc: Version nouvelle présentée et ordonnée par Robert Brasillach.* Paris: Librairie de la Revue Francaise, 1932.

ITALIAN

Cremisi, Teresa. *Rouen 1431 [i.e. millequattrocentotrentuno]: Il processo di condanna di Giovanna d'Arco.* [Milan]: Guanda, 1977.

GERMAN

Schirmer-Imhoff, Ruth. *Der Prozess Jeanne d'Arc: Akten und Protokolle, 1431–1456.* Ungekürtze Ausg. Munich: Deutscher Taschenbuch Verlag, 1963. Selections translated from Latin and French documents.

Rehabilitation

FRENCH AND LATIN

Duparc, Pierre, and Société de l'histoire de France. *Procès en nullité de la condamnation de Jeanne d'Arc.* 5 vols. Paris: Klincksieck, 1977.

Estouteville, Guillaume d', Cardinal. *La réhabilitation de Jeanne la Pucelle: L'enquête du cardinal d'Es touteville en 1452.* Paris: Librairie d'Argences, 1958.

Doncoeur, Paul, and Yvonne Lanhers, eds. *La réhabilitation de Jeanne la Pucelle: L'enquête ordonnée par Charles VII en 1450 et le codicille de Guillaume Bouillé.* Paris: Librairie d'Argences, 1956 (Documents et recherches relatifs à Jeanne la Pucelle 3).

Fabre, Joseph. *Procès de réhabilitation de Jeanne d'Arc: Raconté et traduit d'après les textes latins officiels, suivi de Jeanne et le peuple de France.* New ed. Paris: Hachette, 1913.

Lanéry d'Arc, Pierre, and Jules Étienne Joseph Quicherat, eds. and comps. *Mémoires et consulations en faveur de Jeanne d'Arc par les juges du procès de rehabilitation d'après les manuscrits authentiques.* Paris: Picard, 1889.

Letters

ENGLISH

Quintal, Claire, and Daniel S. Rankin. *Letters of Joan of Arc.* Pittsburgh: Pittsburgh Diocesan Council of Catholic Women, 1969.

Murray, T. Douglas, et al., eds. *Jeanne d'Arc, Maid of Orleans, Deliverer of France.* New York: McClure, Phillips and Co., 1902.

FRENCH

Doncoeur, Paul. *Paroles et lettres de Jeanne la Pucelle.* Paris: Plon, 1960.

Roessler, Charles. *L'armure et les lettres de Jeanne d'Arc: Documents conservés à l'Abbay de Saint-Denis et aux archives de la famille d'Arc du Lys.* Paris: Picard, 1910.

DUTCH AND MIDDLE FRENCH

Winter, Johanna Maria van, and D. Th. Enklaar. *De brieven van Jeanne d'Arc.* Groningen: Wolters, 1954 (Fontes minores medii aevi 1). Correspondence in Middle French.

SELECTIONS

"Joan of Arc." In Serinity Young, ed., *An Anthology of Sacred Texts by and about Women,* pp. 81–83.
Juana de Arco. 1st ed. Mexico City: Publicaciones Cruz O, 1982.
Trask, Willard, ed. and trans. *Joan of Arc, Self Portrait.* New York: Stackpole, 1936; reprint, Collier Books, 1961.

Chapter 8

Fourteenth- and Fifteenth-Century Mystics and Women of the Court

Bridget of Sweden (1303–73)

Wealthy, a mother of eight, Bridget was widowed at the age of forty when her husband died after their return from a pilgrimage to Spain. This made it possible for her to abandon her ties to the world and devote herself to religion. She founded the religious order of the Brigittines. These had dual monasteries of women and men that shared a chapel. They were particularly devoted to learning. Bridget spent a substantial part of her later years in Rome, seeking approval for her new order. She assisted Catherine of Siena in achieving the return of the papacy from Avignon to Rome. The revelations that Bridget received were widely published and respected throughout the later Middle Ages.

Revelations

ENGLISH

Harris, Marguerite Tjader, ed., and Albert Ryle Kezel, trans. *Life and Selected Revelations*. New York: Paulist Press, 1990 (Classics of Western Spirituality). Translation of: *Revelationes*, bks. 5 and 7, and the four prayers from the *Revelationes*.

Graf, Ernest. *Selections*. New York: Benziger Brothers, 1928.

MIDDLE ENGLISH

Ellis, Roger, ed. *The Liber celestis of St. Bridget of Sweden: The Middle English Version in British Library MS Claudius B i, together with a Life of the Saint from the Same Manuscript.* Oxford and New York: Oxford University Press, 1987. Middle English text is translated from the Latin.

Cumming, William Patterson, ed. *The Revelations of Saint Birgitta.* Oxford: Oxford University Press, 1929 (Early English Text Society [original series] 178); reprint, New York: Kraus Reprint, 1971.

SELECTIONS

Kezel, Albert R. "Birgitta of Sweden, *Revelations.*" In Amy G. Oden, ed., *In Her Words: Women's Writings in the History of Christian Thought,* pp. 170–80.

SWEDISH

Bergh, Birger, ed. *Sancta Birgitta Revelaciones.* Uppsala: Almqvist and Wiksell, 1967– (Samlingar utgivna av Svenska fornskriftsällskapet, ser. 2, Latinska skrifter 7/1–5). Summary in English.

Lundén, Tryggve. *Himmelska uppenbarelser.* Malmö: Allhems Förlag, 1957.

Hollman, Lennart, ed. *Den Heliga Birgittas Reuelaciones extrauagantes.* Uppsala: Almqvist and Wiksell, 1956 (Samlingar utgivna av Svenska fornskriftsällskapet, ser. 2, Latinsk a skrifter 5). Summary in English.

Skovgaard, Johanne. *Den hellige Birgitta/kilderne til hendes historie og udvalg af hen des skrifter i oversaettelse ved Johanne Skovgaard.* Copenhagen: Schønberg, 1921.

Steffen, Richard. *Den heliga Birgittas uppenbarelser i urval och öfversättning; med inledning, anmärkningar och förklaringar.* Stockholm, 1909.

Klemming, G. E., and Vadsterna Birgittasystrarna. *Heliga Birgittas uppenbarelser.* Stockholm: Norstedt, 1857. Vol. 5 (*Bihang*) contains *Stadgar för Vadstena kloster: Ett bref från Birgitta till sonen Birger.*

OTHER WORKS

Bridgettine Breviary

Officium parvum beate Marie Virginis = Vår Frus tidegärd. Uppsala: University of Uppsala; and Stockholm: Almqvist and Wiksell, distr., 1976 (Acta Universitatis Upsaliensis; Studia historicoecclesiastica Upsaliensia 27–28). Latin and/or Swedish; with Psalms identified by number and initial words only. Summary in English.

Eklund, Sten. *Opera minora.* Stockholm: Almqvist and Wiksell, 1975. Text in Latin, introduction in English. At head of title: Kungl. vitterhets historie och antikvitets Akademien, Stockholm.

The Fifteen 0's: And Other Prayers. London: Griffith and Farran, 1869.

Catherine of Siena (1347–80)

Catherine was a member of the Dominican Third Order (lay religious living in the world) from the age of sixteen. She had received visions since her childhood. She lived a very holy life: in contemplative prayer; working with the poor and sick; and converting sinners. She had many followers during her lifetime and exercised substantial influence, including persuading Pope Gregory XI to return the papacy to Rome from its seventy-year exile in Avignon. A number of her influential letters have been preserved as well as the *Dialogue* and some prayers. In 1970, she was one of the first women to be recognized as a Doctor of the Church by the Roman Catholic Church.

Collections of Works

ENGLISH

Noffke, Suzanne. *The Texts and Concordances of the Works of Caterina da Siena.* Microfiche. Madison, Wis.: Hispanic Seminary of Medieval Studies, 1987. Text in Italian; guide in English.

SELECTIONS (ENGLISH)

Berrigan, Joseph, trans. "The Tuscan Visionary: Saint Catherine of Siena." In Katharina M. Wilson, ed., *Medieval Women Writers,* pp. 252–68.

Foster, Kenelm, and Mary John Ronayne. *I, Catherine: Selected Writings of St. Catherine of Siena.* London: Collins, 1980.

Noffke, Suzanne, O.P., trans. "Catherine of Siena." In Serinity Young, ed., *An Anthology of Sacred Texts by and about Women,* pp. 75–76.

———. "Catherine of Siena, *Dialogue.*" In Amy G. Oden, ed., *In Her Words: Women's Writings in the History of Christian Thought,* pp. 187–203.

———. "From Prayer 20." In Jane Hirshfield, ed., *Women in Praise of the Sacred*, pp. 116–17.

Petroff, Elizabeth, trans. "Letters." In Elizabeth Petroff, ed., *Medieval Women's Visionary Literature*, pp. 263–75.

Scudder, V. D., trans. "Persuading a Pope." In Barbara J. MacHaffie, ed., *Readings in Her Story*, pp. 65–67.

SELECTIONS (ITALIAN)

Piccari, Tarsicio. *Caterina da Siena, mistica illetterata*. Torino: Paoline, 1991 (I Tascabili dello spirito 5). "Testi antologici scelti" — Pp. [153]–252.

Di Ciaccia, Giuseppe. *Passione per la Chiesa: Scritti scelti*. Rome: Città Nuova, 1989.

ITALIAN

Riccardi, Carlo, ed. *Messaggio di Santa Caterina da Siena, dottore della Chiesa: Tutto il pensiero della Vergine Senese esposto con le sue parole in forma moderna*. 2d ed. Rome: C.L.V., 1988. Preface by Giuliana Cavallini.

SPANISH

Salvador y Conde, José. *Obras de Santa Catalina de Siena: El Diálogo, Oraciones y Soliloquíos*. Madrid: Editorial Católica, 1980.

Letters

ITALIAN

Noffke, Suzanne. *The Letters of St. Catherine of Siena*. Binghamton, N.Y.: Medieval and Renaissance Texts and Studies, 1988 (Medieval and Renaissance Texts and Studies 52).

Scudder, Vida Dutton. *Saint Catherine of Siena as Seen in Her Letters*. London: J. M. Dent; New York: Dutton, 1905.

ITALIAN

Pensabene, Giuseppe. *Lettere a papi e a cardinali*. Rome: Volpe, 1968.

Duprè Theseider, Eugenio. *Epistolario*. Torino: Bottega d'Erasmo, 1966 (Fonti per la storia d'Italia; Epistolari, sec. 14; no. 82). Reprint of: Rome: Istituto Storico Italiano per il Medio Evo, 1966.

————. *Epistolario di Santa Caterina da Siena*. Rome: Tipografia del Senato, 1940.

Lettere di Santa Caterina da Siena agli artisti e ai professionisti. Rome: Palombi, 1939.

Tommaseo, Niccolo, and Saverio Fino. *Lettere scelte*. Torino: Unione Tipografico-editrice Torinese, 1920 (Collezione di classici italiani 17).

Ferretti, Lodovico. *Lettere di S. Caterina da Siena: Vergine domenicana*. Siena: Tip. S. Caterina, 1918.

Tommaseo, Niccolo, and Piero Misciatelli. *Le lettere*. 3d ed. Siena: Giuntini Bentivoglio, 1913. Vol. 6 entitled: *Le lettere di S. Caterina da Siena e di alcuni suoi discepoli*.

SPANISH

Salvador y Conde, José. *Ideario y vida de Catalina de Siena: Doctora de la iglesia*. Salamanca: Editorial San Esteban, 1990 (Biblioteca dominicana 9).

————. *Epistolario de Santa Catalina de Siena: Espiritualidad y doctrinas*. Salamanca: Editorial San Esteban, 1982 (Biblioteca dominicana 1).

FRENCH

Lettres de Sainte Catherine de Sienne. Paris: P. Téqui, 1977 (Livre d'or des écrits mystiques). Reprint of the 1886 ed. published by Poussielgue, Paris.

Prayers (*Le orazioni*)

ENGLISH

Noffke, Suzanne. *The Prayers of Catherine of Siena*. New York: Paulist Press, 1983.

ITALIAN

L'oratorio di Santa Caterina in Fontebranda: Le vicende costruttive, gli affreschi, gli argenti. Siena: Nobile Contrada dell'Oca, 1990.

Dialogue (Libro della divina dottrina)

ENGLISH

Noffke, Suzanne. *The Dialogue.* New York: Paulist Press, 1980 (Classics of Western Spirituality).

Hodgson, Phyllis, and Gabriel Michael Liegey, ed. *The Orcherd of Syon.* London: Published for the Early English Text Society by the Oxford University Press, 1966.

Thorold, Algar Labouchere, ed. and trans. *The Dialogue of the Seraphic Virgin, Catherine of Siena Dictated by Her, While in a State of Ecstasy, to Her Secretaries, and Completed in the Year of Our Lord 1370. Together with an Account of Her Death by an Eye-witness.* New and abridged ed. Westminster, Md.: Newman, 1944.

ITALIAN

Raschini, Maria Adelaide, and Gabriella Anodal, eds. *Dialogo della divina Provvidenza.* Bologna: Studio domenicano, 1989 (Collana attendite ad detram 3). Modern Italian version of *Libro della divina dottrina.*

Meattini, Umberto. *Il Libro.* Alba: Edizioni Paoline, 1975 (Collana patristica e del pensiero cristiano).

Gallarati-Scotti, Tommaso conte, ed. *Le più belle pagine di Caterina da Siena.* Milan: Fratelli Treves, 1922.

Fiorilli, Matilde. *Libro della divina dottrina: Volgarmente detto Dialogo della divina provvidenza.* New ed. Bari: G. Laterza, 1912.

Julian of Norwich (1343–after 1413)

Julian lived alone, as an anchoress attached to Saint Julian's church in Norwich, England. Little else is known of her life except for her writings. It is probable that she was well known as a spiritual counselor and was visited by Margery Kempe. Her *Revelations,* or *Showings,* were written in two different editions, the (earlier) Short Text and the (later) Long Text. They have been widely read and have been noted for their use of feminine imagery for God.

MODERN ENGLISH

Walsh, James. *The Revelations of Divine Love of Julian of Norwich*. Wheathampstead: Anthony Clarke Books, 1980.

Watkin, Edward Ingram. *On Julian of Norwich; and in Defence of Margery Kempe*. Exeter and Devon: University of Devon, 1979 (Exeter Medieval English Texts and Studies).

Colledge, Edmund, and James Walsh, trans. *Showings*. New York: Paulist Press, 1978 (Classics of Western Spirituality).

Del Mastro, M. L. *Revelations of Divine Love*. Garden City, N.Y.: Image Books, 1977.

Cooper, Austin. *Julian of Norwich: Reflections on Selected Texts*. North American ed.: Mystic, Conn.: Twenty-Third Publications, 1988. "Originally published in Australia, copyright 1986; published in Great Britain in 1987 by Burns and Oates, Ltd, Tunbridge Wells, Kent."

Doyle, Brendan. *Meditations with Julian of Norwich*. Santa Fe, N.M.: Bear and Co., 1983.

Wolters, Clifton, trans. *Revelations of Divine Love*. New York: Penguin, 1966.

Walsh, James, trans. *The Revelations of Divine Love of Julian of Norwich*. London: Burns and Oates, 1961.

———. *The Revelations of Divine Love of Julian of Norwich*. St. Meinrad, Ind.: Abbey Press, 1961 (Religious Experience series 3).

Chambers, Percy Franklin. *Juliana of Norwich: An Introductory Appreciation and an Interpretative Anthology*. New York: Harper and Brothers, 1955. Also London: Gollanz.

Hudleston, Gilbert Roger, ed. *Revelations of Divine Love Shewed to a Devout Ankress*. 2d ed. London: Burns and Oates; Westminster, Md.: Newman Press, 1952 (Orchard Books 11). "In the present edition the text has been based upon ms. Sloane 2499."

Cressy, Serenus, and George Tyrrell. *XVI Revelations of Divine Love Shewed to Mother Juliana of Norwich 1373*. London: Kegan Paul, Trench, Trübner, 1920.

Revelations of Divine Love Shewed to Mother Juliana of Norwich, 1373. St. Louis: Herder, 1920.

Warrack, Grace Harriet, ed. *Revelations of Divine Love, Recorded by Julian, Anchoress at Norwich, Anno Domini 1373: A Version from the Ms. in the British Museum*. London: Methuen and Company, Ltd, 1901.

Sixteen Revelations of Divine Love Made to a Devout Servant of Our Lord, Called Mother Juliana, an Anchorete of Norwich, Who Lived in the Days of King Edward the Third. Boston: Ticknor and Fields, 1864.

CRITICAL EDITION

Colledge, Edmund, and James Walsh, eds. *A Book of Showings to the Anchoress Julian of Norwich.* Toronto: Pontifical Institute of Mediaeval Studies, 1978 (Studies and Texts 35).

MIDDLE ENGLISH

Glasscoe, Marion, ed. *A Revelation of Love.* Exeter: University of Exeter, 1976 (Exeter Medieval English Texts and Studies). Middle English text, modern English introduction and notes. Rev. ed., 1993.
Beer, Frances, ed. *Julian of Norwich's Revelations of Divine Love: The Shorter Version Ed. from B.L. Add. MS 37790.* Heidelberg: Winter, 1978 (Middle English Texts 8).

FRENCH

Renaudin, Paul, ed. *Mystiques anglais: Richard Rolle, Juliane de Norwich, le Nuage de l'inconnaissance, Walter Hilton.* Paris: Aubier, Éditions Montaigne, 1957.

SELECTIONS

"An Anchoress of England: Julian of Norwich." In Marcelle Thiébaux, trans., *The Writings of Medieval Women,* 2d ed., pp. 441–65.
Colledge, Edmund, and J. Walsh, trans. "Showings (Long Text)." In Elizabeth Petroff, ed., *Medieval Women's Visionary Literature,* pp. 308–13.
Del Mastro, M. L., trans. "Jesus as Mother." In Barbara J. MacHaffie, ed., *Readings in Her Story,* pp. 63–65.
"An English Anchoress: Julian of Norwich." In Marcelle Thiébaux, trans., *The Writings of Medieval Women,* pp. 221–34.
Wolters, Clifton, trans. "Julian of Norwich, *Showings.*" In Amy G. Oden, ed., *In Her Words: Women's Writings in the History of Christian Thought,* pp. 181–86.

Margery Kempe (1373–1439)

Margery was born at Lynn, in Norfolk, England, daughter of a man who was sometimes mayor of the town. She was married to John Kempe and had fourteen children. All that is known of her comes from the book she dictated. She began having visions after a bout of madness in 1413. She was very ardent in condemning all forms of pleasure, to the point that townsfolk accused her of Lollardy. Shortly after, she and her husband took vows of chastity. Margery made a number of pilgrimages that are a major feature of her book, and she tells of visiting Julian of Norwich for encouragement and confirmation of her visions.

CRITICAL EDITION

Meech, Sanford B., ed. and Hope Emily Allen. *The Book of Margery Kempe*. London: Printed for the Early English Text Society by Oxford University Press, 1940; reprint, 1961 (Early English Text Society [original series] 212).

ENGLISH

The Book of Margery Kempe. Harmondsworth, Eng., and New York: Penguin, 1985 (Penguin Classics).

Crawford, Charles, and Henry Pepwell. *The Cell of Self-Knowledge: Early English Mystical Treatises*. New York: Crossroad, 1981 (Spiritual Classics). "Title selected by the editor [Edmund G. Gardner] of the second edition of the present collection of Middle English treatises, first published by Henry Pepwell in London in 1521."

Collis, Louise. *Memoirs of a Medieval Woman: The Life and Times of Margery Kempe*. New York: Crowell, 1964. Originally published in England in 1964 under title *The Apprentice Saint*.

Butler-Bowdon, William. *The Book of Margery Kempe, 1436*. London: J. Cape, 1936. Later editions with various imprints.

SELECTIONS

Butler-Bowdon, W., trans. "Margery Kempe." In Barbara J. MacHaffie, ed., *Readings in Her Story*, pp. 61–63.

Dickman, Susan, trans. "From 'The Book of Margery Kempe.'" In Elizabeth Petroff, ed., *Medieval Women's Visionary Literature*, pp. 314–29.

"Four English Women of the Fifteenth Century: Margery Kempe; Julians Barnes; Queen Margaret of Anjou; Margery Brews Paston." In Marcelle Thiébaux, trans., *The Writings of Medieval Women,* 2d ed., pp. 467–523 (*Boke of Margery Kempe,* pp. 488–503).

Hawker, Gillian. *The Mirror of Love.* London: Darton, Longman and Todd, 1988.

The Mirror of Love: Readings with Margery Kempe. Harrisburg, Pa.: Morehouse, 1991.

Florencia Pinar

Florencia was a woman of the nobility from late fifteenth-century Spain. Three of her poems survive and can be found in the *Cancionero general,* compiled by Hernando del Castillo.

Snow, Joseph, trans. "The Spanish Love Poet: Florencia Pinar." In Katharina M. Wilson, ed., *Medieval Women Writers,* pp. 320–32.

Rodríguez Moñino, Antonio R., ed. *Cancionero general.* Madrid, 1958.

Rodríguez Moñino, Antonio R., ed. Hernando del Castillo, *Segunda parte del Cancionero general: Agora nuevamente copilado de lo mas gracioso y discreto de muchos afamados trovadores (Zaragoza, 1552).* Oxford: Dolphin Book Co.; Valencia: Castalia, 1956 (Floresta, joyas poéticas españolas 7).

Leonora López de Córdoba (1362–1412)

A memoir of Leonora survives in which she describes the sufferings of herself and her family. They were prosperous gentry of Córdoba but lost everything when the military fortunes of their party were reversed. Leonora, her husband, and her whole family were put in prison, where most of her family died of the plague. She and her husband eventually were released and gained some measure of restoration of fortunes, although Leonora's position as lady-in-waiting to the queen of Castile did not last, and she retired to a convent.

Lacy, Kathleen, trans. "The Memories of Doña Leonor López de Córdoba." In Elizabeth Petroff, ed., *Medieval Women's Visionary Literature,* pp. 329–34.

Ayerba-Chaux, Reinaldo. "Las memorias de Doña Leonor López de Córdoba." *Journal of Hispanic Philology* 2 (1977) pp. 11–33.

Christine de Pisan (c. 1363–c. 1431)

Christine was born in Italy but grew up in the French court of Charles V where her father was a court astrologer and physician. She married Étienne de Castel while she was in her teens, and they had three children. When Étienne died around 1390, Christine needed to support her family. With her excellent education and contacts at court, she was able to make a successful career as a writer. She wrote an extensive corpus of books and poetry dealing largely with medieval values and ideals, particularly with the obligations and dignity of women. She defended women against the satire of Jean de Meun in his version of the *Roman de la rose.* Christine's last years were spent in the convent of Poissy.

SECONDARY WORKS

Richards, Earl Jeffrey, ed. *Reinterpreting Christine de Pizan.* Athens: University of Georgia Press, 1992.

Willard, Charity Cannon. *Christine de Pizan: Her Life and Works: A Biography.* New York: Persea Books, 1984.

BIBLIOGRAPHIES OF WORKS BY AND ABOUT CHRISTINE

Yenal, Edith. *Christine de Pisan: A Bibliography.* Metuchen, N.J.: Scarecrow Press, 1989 (Scarecrow Author Bibliographies 63).

Kennedy, Angus J. *Christine de Pizan: A Bibliographical Guide.* London: Grant and Cutler, 1984.

SELECTIONS

"Poet of the Court of France: Christine de Pizan." In Marcelle Thiébaux, trans., *The Writings of Medieval Women,* pp. 235–50.

Richards, Earl Jeffrey, trans. "Christine de Pizan." In Serinity Young, ed., *An Anthology of Sacred Texts by and about Women*, pp. 76–78.

Willard, Charity Cannon. "The Franco-Italian Professional Writer: Christine de Pizan." In Katharina M. Wilson, ed., *Medieval Women Writers*, pp. 333–64.

———, ed. *The Writings of Christine de Pizan*. New York: Persea Books, 1994.

"A Woman of Letters at the French Court: Christine de Pizan." In Marcelle Thiébaux, trans., *The Writings of Medieval Women*, 2d ed., pp. 413–40.

Poetry

SELECTIONS

Margolis, Nadia, trans. "The One Hundred Ballads (1393–1399?)." In Elizabeth Petroff, ed., *Medieval Women's Visionary Literature*, pp. 339–40.

ENGLISH

Margolis, Nadia. *The Lyric Poetry of Christine de Pizan*. New York: Garland, 1987.

FRENCH

Püschel, Robert. *Le livre du chemin de long estude; publié pour la première fois d'après sept manuscrits de Paris, de Bruxelles et de Berlin*. Berlin: Damköhler, [1887].

Rains, Ruth Rea Ringland, ed. *Les sept psaumes allégorisés: A Critical Ed. from the Brussels and Paris Manuscripts*. Washington, D.C.: Catholic University of America Press, 1965.

Roy, Maurice, ed. *Oeuvres poétiques de Christine de Pisan*. Paris: Firmin Didot et Cie, 1886.

Varty, Kenneth, ed. *Ballades, Rondeaux, and Virelais: An Anthology*. Leicester: Leicester University Press, 1965. Poems in French.

Romance of the Rose Debate

ÉPISTRE DU DIEU D'AMOURS (1399)

Hoccleve, Thomas, et al. *Poems of Cupid: God of Love.* Leiden and
New York: Brill, 1990. Poems in Old French and Middle English
with English translations on parallel pages.

ENGLISH

Ward, Charles Frederick, Jean Gerson, and Pierre Col. "The Epistles on
the *Romance of the Rose* and Other Documents in the Debate."
Ph.D. diss., University of Chicago, 1911.

SELECTION

Margolis, Nadia, trans. "Christine's Response to the Treatise on the *Romance of the Rose* by John Montrevil, June–July 1401: The First
Extant Combative Document in the Debate." In Elizabeth Petroff,
ed., *Medieval Women's Visionary Literature,* pp. 340–46.

FRENCH

Hicks, Eric. *Le débat sur le "Roman de la rose."* Paris: H. Champion,
1977. French, Old French, or Latin.
Beck, Friedrich. *Les épistres sur le "Roman de la rose."* Neuburg a. D:
Griessmayer, 1888.

Le livre de la cité des dames (1405)

ENGLISH

Richards, Earl Jeffrey, trans. *The Book of the City of Ladies.* 1st ed.
New York: Persea Books, 1982.

FRENCH

Hicks, Eric, and Thérèse Moreau. *Le livre de la cité des dames.* Paris:
Stock, 1986 (Série "Moyen Age"). Cover title: *La cité des dames.*
Cerquiglini, Jacqueline. *Cent ballades d'amant et de dame.* Paris: Union
Générale d'Éditions, 1982 (Bibliothèque médievale).
Curnow, Maureen Cheney, ed. "The *Livre de la cité des dames* of Chris-
tine de Pisan." Ph.D. diss., Vanderbilt University, 1975. Text in

French; introduction and editorial matter in English. Available from University Microfilms International.

Livre des trois vertus (1406)

ENGLISH

Cosman, Madelein P., ed., and Charity Cannon Willard, trans. *A Medieval Woman's Mirror of Honor: The Treasury of the City of Ladies.* New York: Bard Hall Press/Persea Books, 1989.

SELECTION

Richards, E. J., trans. "Virtuous Women." In Barbara J. MacHaffie, ed., *Readings in Her Story.*

FRENCH

Willard, Charity Cannon, and Eric Hicks. *Le livre des trois vertus.* Critical ed. Paris: H. Champion, 1989 (Bibliothèque du XVe siècle 50). Middle French text, with introduction and notes in French.

PORTUGUESE

O espelho de Cristina. Lisbon: Ministério da Educação e Cultura, Secretaria de Estado da Cultura, Biblioteca Nacional, 1987. Facsimile reprint of: Lisbon: G. de Campos, 1518 ed.

Carstens-Grokenberger, Dorothee. *Buch von den drei Tugenden: In portugiesischer übersetzung.* Münster: Aschendorffsche Verlagsbuchhandlungen, 1961 (Portugiesische Forschungen der Görresgesellschaft Reihe 2, vol. 1).

Lavision de Christine (1405)

McLeod, Glenda K., trans. *Christine's Vision: Christine de Pizan.* New York: Garland, 1993 (Garland Library of Medieval Literature 68, series B).

Margolis, Nadia, trans. "Selections from the Works of Christine de Pizan: The Lavision-Christine." In Elizabeth Petroff, ed., *Medieval Women's Visionary Literature,* pp. 335–39.

Towner, Mary Louis, Sister. *Pizan's Lavision-Christine.* New York: AMS Press, 1969. Text in French. Reprint of the edition published in Washington, D.C., 1932.

Livre de faits et bonnes meurs du sage roi Charles V (1404)

FRENCH

Solente, Suzanne, ed. *Le livre des fais et bonnes meurs du sage roy Charles V.* Paris: H. Champion, 1936; reprinted 1977.

Michaud, J. F., ed. *Le livre des fais et bonnes meurs du sage roy Charles V.* In *Nouvelle collection des mémoires pour servir à l'histoire de France.* Paris, 1836–39, 1:581–637, 2:1–202.

Petitot, Claude B, ed. *Le livre des fais et bonnes meurs du sage roy Charles V.* In *Collection complète des mémoires relatifs à l'histoire de France.* Paris, 1819–29, 5:200, 6:146.

Livre de paix

FRENCH AND ENGLISH

Willard, Charity Cannon, ed. *The "Livre de la paix."* The Hague: Mouton, 1958. Critical edition with introduction and notes by Charity Cannon Willard; introductory material and notes in English; text in French.

Le livre des fais du bon messire Jehan Le Maingre

ENGLISH

Kennedy, Angus J. and Kenneth Varty, eds. *Ditié de Jehanne d'Arc [by] Christine de Pisan; edited by Angus J. Kennedy and Kenneth Varty.* Oxford: Society for the Study of Mediaeval Languages and Literature, 1977 (Medium Ævum monographs; n.s., /9/9/). English and Middle French text; English introduction and notes; bibliography: pp. 75–80.

FRENCH

Cardoze, Michel. *Jeanne d'Arc: Dossier non classé.* Paris: Librairie Seguier, 1987. "Le ditié de Christine de Pisan": pp. 163–81.

Lalande, Denis. *Le livre des fais du bon messire Jehan Le Maingre, dit Bouciquaut, mareschal de France et gouverneur de Jennes.* Geneva: Droz, 1985 (Textes littéraires français 331).

Le livre du duc des vrais amants

ENGLISH

Fenster, Thelma S., and Nadia Margolis. *The Book of the Duke of True Lovers.* New York: Persea Books, 1991.

Welch, Alice Kemp, ed., and Laurence Binyon and Eric R. D. Maclagan, trans. *The Book of the Duke of True Lovers: Now First Translated from the Middle French of Christine de Pisan.* London: Chatto and Windus, 1908 (Medieval library 1).

CRITICAL EDITION

Fenster, Thelma S., ed. *Le livre du duc des vrais amans.* Binghamton, N.Y.: Medieval and Renaissance Texts and Studies, 1994 (Medieval and Renaissance Texts and Studies 124).

Fate of Arms and Chivalry

ENGLISH

The Fayt of Armes & of Chyualrye. Amsterdam: Theatrum Orbis Terrarum; New York: Da Capo Press, 1968 (The English Experience, Its Record in Early Printed Books Published in Facsimile, no. 13). Facsimile of the Westminster ed. of 1489, translated and printed by William Caxton.

The Book of Fayttes of Armes and of Chyualrye. London: Published for the Early English Text Society by H. Milford, Oxford University Press, 1932 (Early English Text Society [original series] 189).

Épître d'Othéa la déese à Hector

ENGLISH

Chance, Jane. *Christine de Pizan's Letter of Othea to Hector: Translated with Introduction, Notes, and Interpretative Essay.* Newburyport, Mass.: Focus Information Group, 1990 (Focus Library of Medieval Women).

Scrope, Stephen, and Curt F. Bühler, trans. and eds. *The Epistle of Othea.* London and New York: Oxford University Press, 1970.

Scrope, Stephen, and George Warner. *The Epistle of Othea to Hector; or, The Boke of Knyghthode.* London: J. B. Nichols and Sons, 1904.

FRENCH

Gheyn, Joseph van den, ed. *Épître d'Othéa, déese de la prudence, à Hector, chef des Troyens; reproduction des 100 miniatures du manuscrit 9392 de Jean Miélot.* Brussels: Vromant and Co., 1913.

Corps de policie

ENGLISH

Forhan, Kate Langdon, trans. *The Book of the Body Politic.* Cambridge and New York: Cambridge University Press, 1994 (Cambridge Texts in the History of Political Thought).

Bornstein, Diane. *The Middle English Translation of Christine de Pisan's Livre du corps de policie: Ed. from MS C.U.L.Kk.1.5. by Diane Bornstein.* Heidelberg: Winter, 1977. Text in Middle English; introductory and explanatory material in modern English; bibliography: pp. 221–24.

The Body of Polycye. Amsterdam: Theatrum Orbis Terrarum; New York: Da Capo Press, 1971 (The English Experience, Its Record in Early Printed Books Published in Facsimile, no. 304). Facsimile of the edition printed in London by J. Scott in 1521.

CRITICAL EDITION

Rucas, Robert Harold, ed. *Le livre du corps de policie.* Geneva: Librairie Droz, 1967 (Textes littéraires français 145).

FRENCH

Solente, Suzanne, ed. *Le livre de la mutacion de fortune.* Paris: Picard, 1959. The present edition is based on MS 9508 in the Bibliothèque Royale de Belgique, Brussels.

Épistre de la prison de vie humaine

FRENCH AND ENGLISH

Wisman, Josette A. *The Epistle of the Prison of Human Life; with, an Epistle to the Queen of France; and, Lament on the Evils of the Civil War.* New York: Garland, 1984. French text, parallel English translation.

Kennedy, Angus J. *Christine de Pizan's "Épistre de la prison de vie humaine."* Glasgow and London: A. J. Kennedy; distributed by Grant and Cutler, 1984.

Helene Kottanner (c. 1400–c. 1452)

Helene was chambermaid to Queen Elizabeth of Hungary. She wrote memoirs that recount her assistance to the queen after the death of Elizabeth's husband Albrecht. In order to secure the throne of Hungary for Elizabeth's infant son (Ladislaus), Helene and Elizabeth stole the holy crown of Saint Stephen and had the child baptized, knighted, and anointed king to ensure his rights against Elizabeth's new husband, the king of Poland. Helene's narrative is a lively account of her adventures and the political intrigues of fifteenth-century Hungary.

SELECTIONS (ENGLISH)

Bijvoet, Maya C., trans. "Helene Kottanner: The Austrian Chambermaid." In Katharina M. Wilson, *Women Writers of the Renaissance and Reformation,* pp. 327–49.

CRITICAL EDITION

Mollay, Karoly, ed. *Die Denkwürdigkeiten der Helene Kottannerin, 1439–1440.* Vienna: Oesterreichischer Bundesverlag für Unterricht, Wissenschaft und Kunst, 1971.

HUNGARIAN

Mollay, Karoly, ed. *A korona elrablasa: Kottanner Janosne emlekirata, 1439/1440.* N.p.: Magyar Helikon, 1978 (Bibliotheca historica).

Catherine of Bologna (1413–63)

Catherine grew up in the court of Ferrara and was a playmate of and then lady-in-waiting to Margaret d'Este. She was well educated and trained in calligraphy and painting miniatures. She gradually became interested in the Franciscan life and was a tertiary for several years before entering a convent of the Poor Clares (the cloistered Franciscan sisters). She had many visions, some of which she considered to be from God and others from the devil. She wrote her *Le armi spirituali* (Weapons of the Spirit) based on these experiences.

SELECTIONS (ENGLISH)

Berrigan, Joseph R., trans. "Saint Catherine of Bologna: Franciscan Mystic." In Katharina M. Wilson, *Women Writers of the Renaissance and Reformation*, pp. 67–80.

SELECTIONS (ITALIAN)

Battelli, Guido, ed. *Le armi spirituali*. Florence: G. Giannini, 1922.

ITALIAN

Foletti, Cecilia, ed. *Le sette armi spirituali*. Padua: Antenore, 1985 (Medioeuoe Umanesimo 56).

Catherine of Genoa (1447–1510)
(Saint Caterina da Genova)

Catherine was born of the nobility and married at age sixteen. Ten years later, she experienced a sudden conversion. She remained married, although her husband's worldliness was difficult for her to bear. Catherine spent much time caring for the sick in a hospital in Genoa. While her husband was eventually converted and became a Franciscan tertiary, Catherine never associated herself with a religious order. Catherine had many extraordinary mental experiences and visions that were studied in an important work by the Roman Catholic modernist theologian Baron Friedrich von Hügel:

Hügel, Friedrich Freiherr von. *The Mystical Element of Religion: As Studied in Saint Catherine of Genoa and Her Friends*. London: J.M. Dent; New York: Dutton, 1908.

ENGLISH

Hughes, Serge, trans. *Purgation and Purgatory: The Spiritual Dialogue.* New York: Paulist Press, 1979 (Classics of Western Spirituality). Introduction by Benedict J. Groeschel, preface by Catherine De Hueck Doherty.

Treatise of S. Catherine of Genoa on Purgatory; Newly Translated by J. M. A.; Edited with an Introductory Essay on Hell and the Intermediate State, by a Priest Associate of the Guild of All-Souls. London: J. Hodges, 1878.

Treatise on Purgatory. London: Burns and Oates; New York: Catholic Publication Society, 1858. New edition, London: Burns, Oates and Washbourne, 1929.

SELECTIONS

Garvin, Paul, trans. *The Life and Sayings of Saint Catherine of Genoa.* Staten Island, N.Y.: Alba House, 1964.

Hughes, Serge, trans. "Catherine of Genoa, *The Spiritual Dialogue.*" In Amy G. Oden, ed., *In Her Words: Women's Writings in the History of Christian Thought,* pp. 204–15.

Nugent, Donald Christopher. "Saint Catherine of Genoa: Mystic of Pure Love." In Katharina M. Wilson, *Women Writers of the Renaissance and Reformation,* pp. 67–80.

CRITICAL EDITION

Bonzi, Umile. *S. Caterina Fieschi Adorno.* 2 vols. Turin: Marietti, 1961–62. Critical edition is in vol. 2.

FRENCH

Debongnie, Pierre, trans. *La grande dame du pur amour, Sainte Catherine de Génes, 1447–1510. Vie et doctrine et Traité du purgatoire.* Paris: Desclée de Brouwer, 1960 (Études carmélitaines).

Bussierre, Marie-Théodore Renouard, trans. *Les oeuvres de Sainte Catherine de Génes, précédés de sa vie par M. Le Vicomte Marie-Théodore de Bussierre.* Paris: A. Tralin, 1926.

Magdalena Beutler (1407–58)

Magdalena was from Freiburg in Germany. She entered a convent of the Poor Clares (cloistered Franciscan nuns) that she struggled to reform to the traditions of Saint Clare and Saint Francis. Magdalena saw visions, received the stigmata, and wrote *Die goldene Litanie* (The golden litany) and *Erklaerung des Vaterunsers* (Meditations on the Pater Noster).

SELECTION

Greenspan, Karen, trans. "From the Life of Magdalena Beutler." In Elizabeth Petroff, ed., *Medieval Women's Visionary Literature,* pp. 350–55.

LETTERS

"Magdalena Beutler." In Wilhelm Oehl, ed., *Deutsche Mystikerbriefe des Mittelalters,* pp. 519–30.

CRITICAL EDITION

Greenspan, Karen, ed. "Erklaerung des Vaterunsers: A Critical Edition of a Fifteenth-century Mystical Treatise." Ph.D. diss., University of Massachusetts at Amherst, 1984. Available from University Microfilms International.

Lidwina von Schiedam (1380–1433)

Lidwina was born in Rotterdam. She refused to marry, preferring to remain a virgin. In her fifteenth year, she fell on ice and broke a rib. From that point on, she was ill for the rest of her life. Despite her own suffering (which increased as her life progressed) Lidwina was concerned with the plight of the poor, giving alms generously, even after she herself was impoverished. She saw visions and received the stigmata. Thomas à Kempis wrote a life of Saint Lidwina.

LETTERS

Oehl, Wilhelm, ed. *Deutsche Mystikerbriefe des Mittelalters,* pp. 493–501.

Chapter 9

Letters and Occasional Writings of the Fifteenth Century

From the late Middle Ages and Renaissance on, letters and occasional writings by women began to survive, at least in manuscript form, in greater and greater numbers. The collections cited below, which contain brief writings by a number of women of the fifteenth century, serve as readily available examples. No effort has been made to comprehensively canvass all the published letters of women of the fourteenth and fifteenth centuries or all the vast amounts of manuscript materials that might yield further letters and other writings by women.

Italian Humanists

Women participated in the cultural awakening of the Italian Renaissance. The collection cited below (King and Rabil, *Her Immaculate Hand*) translates the writings of a number of women and men of interest to women's studies from editions of the seventeenth and eighteenth centuries. Most of these were preserved as a result of being included in the published correspondence of well-known men. The women who wrote letters or speeches included are listed below. Page numbers refer to:

King, Margaret L., and Albert Rabil, eds. *Her Immaculate Hand: Selected Works by and about the Women Humanists of Quattrocento Italy.* Binghamton, N.Y.: Center for Medieval and Early Renaissance Studies, 1983 (Medieval and Renaissance Texts and Studies 20).

Maddalena Scrovegni (1356–1429) pp. 33–35

Battista da Montefeltro
Malatesta (fifteenth century, first half) pp. 35–38

Costanza Varano
(mid–fifteenth century) pp. 39–44, 53–54, 55–56

Ippolita Sforza (1445–?) pp. 44–46

Cassandra Fedele (1465–1556) pp. 48–50, 69–73, 74–77

Issota Nogarola pp. 57–69

Laura Cereta (1469–?) pp. 77–80, 81–84, 85–86

ADDITIONAL SOURCE

Rabil, Albert, ed. *Laura Cereta, Quattrocento Humanist*. Binghamton, N.Y.: Center for Medieval and Early Renaissance Studies, 1981 (Medieval and Renaissance Texts and Studies 3).

Letters

LETTERS FROM THE FRENCH AND ENGLISH COURTS

Bréquigny, Louis Georges Oudart-Deudrix de, comp. *Lettres de rois reines et autres personnages des cours de France et d'Angleterre, depuis Louis VII jusqu'à Henri IV.* Paris: Imprimerie Royale, 1839–47, 1:1162–1300; 2:1301–1515.

Adele of Champagne vol. I, pp. 6–7

Alix of Brittany vol. I, pp. 178–79, 275

Eleanor of Provence
(also in Green [see below]) vol. 1, pp. 245, 264–65, 306–7

LETTERS OF ROYAL AND ILLUSTRIOUS LADIES
OF GREAT BRITAIN

Green, Mary Anne Everett Wood, ed. *Letters of Royal and Illustrious Ladies of Great Britain.* Vol. 1. London, 1846.

ADDITIONAL SOURCES

"Queen of the English People: Matilda, Wife of Henry I." In Marcelle Thiébaux, trans., *The Writings of Medieval Women*, pp. 165–79.
"Good Queen Maud: Matilda, Queen of the English people." In Marcelle Thiébaux, trans., *The Writings of Medieval Women*, 2d ed., pp. 293–313.

ANGLO-NORMAN LETTERS AND PETITIONS FROM ALL SOULS

Legge, M. Dominica. *Anglo-Norman Letters and Petitions from All Souls Ms. 182.* Oxford: Anglo-Norman Text Society by B. H. Blackwell, 1941.

PETITION

LETTERS

Joan, Duchess of Brittany

A Countess to the Queen of England, Her Aunt

ADDITIONAL SOURCE

"Four English Women of the Fifteenth Century: Margery Kempe; Julians Barnes; Queen Margaret of Anjou; Margery Brews Paston." In Marcelle Thiébaux, trans., *The Writings of Medieval Women,* 2d ed., pp. 467–523.

PASTON LETTERS

The Paston family archive yields a fascinating portrait of a fifteenth-century English family. Among the letters that have been preserved are a number written by women. The most prominent among these is Margaret Paston, the wife of John Paston, the head of the family during the time best documented by these letters. The names listed below appear in the index to the Warrington edition of the letters.

Margaret Paston

Dame Elizabeth Brews

Dame Elizabeth Brown

Alice Crane

Cecily Dawn

Elizabeth Mundeford

Agnes Paston

Margery Paston

Elizabeth, Duchess of Suffolk

Elizabeth, Countess of Surrey

Anne Paston and Elizabeth Howard, countess of Oxford, are also in Green (see above).

Virgoe, Roger. *Illustrated Letters of the Paston Family: Private Life in the Fifteenth Century.* London: Macmillan, 1989. American ed.: *Private Life in the Fifteenth Century: Illustrated Letters of the Paston Family.* New York: Weidenfeld and Nicolson, 1989. An illustrated and annotated selection of the letters.

Barber, Richard W. *The Pastons: A Family in the Wars of the Roses.* London: Folio Society, 1981.

Gairdner, James, ed. *The Paston Letters, A.D. 1422–1509.* New complete library ed. London: Chatto and Windus, 1904; New York: AMS Press, 1973. First published in 1874.

Davis, Norman, ed. *Paston Letters and Papers of the Fifteenth Century.* In 3 pts. Oxford: Clarendon, 1971.

Warrington, John. *The Paston Letters.* Rev. ed. London: Dent; New York: Dutton, 1956.

Fenn, John, and Laura Archer-Hind. *The Paston Letters.* London: Dent; New York: Dutton, 1951. "First published in this edition 1924."

Fenn, John, and Alexander Ramsay, eds. *Paston Letters: Original Letters Written during the Reign of Henry VI, Edward IV, and Richard III by Various Persons of Rank or Consequence...with Notes Historical and Explanatory.* New ed. London: Bohn, 1849.

THE STONOR LETTERS AND PAPERS

Kingsford, Charles Lethbridge, ed. *The Stonor Letters and Papers, 1290–1483.* London: Royal Historical Society, 1919 (Camden 3d series 29–30). In the following list, the date of the document(s) is given first, then the document number and page number in vol. 29.

Eleanor le Despenser   c. 1326: no. 3, p. 3

Margaret, Countess of Devon   c. 1380: no. 38, pp. 27–28

Alys, Lady Sudely   before 1431: no. 53, p. 47

Jane Stonor   1463, 1470: nos. 70, 106, pp. 62–63, 109–10
                    c. 1472, 1475: nos. 120, 158, pp. 122–23, 165

Margery Hampden   c. 1465: no. 75, pp. 69–70

Dame Katherine Arundell   c. 1473: no. 125, pp. 128–29

Alice, Duchess of Suffolk   c. 1475: no. 148, p. 154

Kingsford, Charles Lethbridge, ed. *Supplementary Stonor Letters and Papers (1314–1482)*. London: Royal Historical Society, 1923 (Camden Miscellany 13/2).

Alice Ydlaye (Idle)   no. 356, p. 18

The Plumpton Correspondence

Stapleton, Thomas, ed. *The Plumpton Correspondence: Written in the Reigns of Edward IV, Richard III, Henry VII, and Henry VIII*. London: Printed for the Camden Society by J. B. Nichols, 1839 (Camden Society Publications 4). Reprints: New York: AMS, 1968; Gloucester, Eng., and Wolfeboro Falls, N.H.: Sutton, 1990 (with new introduction by Keith Dockray).

Elizabeth Greene   c. 1496: no. 51, p. 80

Writings Not Published since 1800

Teresa (Queen of Portugal) (1075–1130)

A letter to her son Alfonso.

Henriquez, C., ed. *Fasciculus sanctorum ordinis Cisterciensis.* Cologne, 1631, 1:314.

Gertrude van Oosten (b. fourteenth century, Delft)

One of the more important Beguines of fourteenth-century Belgium.

"Asceses seu Exercitia quaedem familiaria." In Joseph Geldolph Ryckel, *Vitae S. Beggae, ducissae Brabantiae andetennensium, Begginarum, et Beggardorum fundatricis.* Louvain, 1631, pp. 362–82.
"Praxis meditationis localis super Passione Domini." In Joseph Geldolph Ryckel, *Vitae S. Beggae, ducissae Brabantiae andetennensium, Begginarum, et Beggardorum fundatricis.* Louvain, 1631, pp. 390–93.
"Vita Gertodis ab Oosten." *Acta sanctorum* 1 (January 6, i) pp. 348–53.

Bibliography

Bibliographies of Related Interest

Affeldt, Werner, and Birgit Dübner-Manthey. *Frauen im Frühmittelalter: Eine Ausgewählte kommentierte Bibliographie.* Frankfurt am Main and New York: P. Lang, 1990.

Bowman, Mary Ann. *Western Mysticism: A Guide to the Basic Works.* Chicago: American Library Association, 1978.

Echols, Anne, and Marty Williams. *The Annotated Index of Medieval Women.* New York: M. Wiener, 1991.

Frederiksen, Elke, ed. *Women Writers of Germany, Austria, and Switzerland: An Annotated Bio-bibliographical Guide.* New York: Greenwood, 1989 (Bibliographies and Indexes in Women's Studies 8).

Gallerstein, Carolyn L., and Kathleen McNerney, eds. *Women Writers of Spain: An Annotated Bio-bibliographical Guide.* New York: Greenwood, 1986 (Bibliographies and Indexes in Women's Studies 2).

Goodwater, Leanna. *Women in Antiquity: An Annotated Bibliography.* Metuchen, N.J.: Scarecrow Press, 1975.

Lagorio, Valerie Marie, and Ritamary Bradley. *The Fourteenth-century English Mystics: A Comprehensive Annotated Bibliography.* New York: Garland, 1981 (Garland Reference Library of the Humanities 190).

Lewis, Gertrud Jaron, Frank Willaert, and Marie José Govers. *Bibliographie zur deutschen Frauenmystik des Mittelalters.* Berlin: Schmidt, 1989 (Bibliographien zur deutschen Literatur des Mittelalters 10).

Saínz y Rodríguez, Pedro. *Introduccíon a la historia de la literatura mística en España.* Madrid: Espasa-Calpe, 1984 (Espasa universitaria Literatura 18).

Sawyer, Michael E., ed. *A Bibliographical Index of Five English Mystics: Richard Rolle, Julian of Norwich, the Author of "The Cloud of Unknowing," Walter Hilton, Margery Kempe.* Pittsburgh: Clifford E. Barbour Library, Pittsburgh Theological Seminary, 1978 (Bibliographia Tripotamopolitana 10).

Sharma, Umesh D., and John Arndt. *Mysticism: A Select Bibliography.* Waterloo, Ont.: Waterloo Lutheran University, 1973.

Smith, Hilda L. *Women and the Literature of the Seventeenth Century: An Annotated Bibliography Based on Wing's Short-title Catalogue.* New York: Greenwood, 1990 (Bibliographies and Indexes in Women's Studies 10).

Wiesner, Merry E. *Women in the Sixteenth Century: A Bibliography.* St. Louis: Center for Information Research, 1983 (Sixteenth Century Bibliography 23).

History of Women

Ariès, Philippe, and Georges Duby, eds. *A History of Private Life.* Cambridge, Mass.: Belknap Press of Harvard University Press, 1987– . Translation of *Histoire de la vie privée.* Volumes:
1. *From Pagan Rome to Byzantium.*
2. *Revelations of the Medieval World.*
3. *Passions of the Renaissance.*
4. *From the Fires of Revolution to the Great War.*
5. *Riddles of Identity in Modern Times.*

Duby, Georges, and Michelle Perrot, gen. eds. *A History of Women in the West.* Cambridge, Mass.: Belknap Press of Harvard University Press, 1992– . Translation of *Storia delle donne in Occidente.* Volumes:
1. *From Ancient Goddesses to Christian Saints.*
2. *Silences of the Middle Ages.*
3. *Renaissance and Enlightenment Paradoxes.*
4. *Emerging Feminism from Revolution to World War.*
5. *Toward a Cultural Identity in the Twentieth Century.*

Lerner, Gerda. *Women and History.* New York and London: Oxford University Press, 1986–93. Volumes:
1. *The Creation of Patriarchy.*
2. *The Creation of Feminist Consciousness: From the Middle Ages to Eighteen-seventy.*

Hagiography

Cazelles, Brigitte. *Lives of Thirteenth-century French Women Saints.* New York: Garland, 1990.

Gehrke, Pamela. *Saints and Scribes: Medieval Hagiography in Its Manuscript Context.* Berkeley: University of California Press, 1993 (University of California Publications in Modern Philology 126).

McNamara, Jo Ann, John E. Halborg, and E. Gordon Whatley. *Sainted Women of the Dark Ages.* Durham, N.C.: Duke University Press, 1992.

Stein, Edith, Lucy Gelber, and Michael Linssen. *The Hidden Life: Hagiographic Essays, Meditations, Spiritual Texts.* Washington, D.C.: ICS, 1992. Translation of *Verborgenes leben.*

Vox benedictina: A Journal of Translations from Monastic Sources. Saskatoon, Sask.: Peregrina, 1984–.

Works about Early Christian Women

Bjerre-Aspegren, Kerstin, and René Kieffer. *The Male Woman: A Feminine Ideal in the Early Church.* Stockholm: Almqvist and Wiksell (distributor), 1990 (Acta Universitatis Upsaliensis. Uppsala Women's Studies. A, Women in Religion 4).

Brock, Sebastian P., and Susan Ashbrook Harvey. *Holy Women of the Syrian Orient.* Berkeley: University of California Press, 1987 (The Transformation of the Classical Heritage).

Burrus, Virginia. *Chastity as Autonomy: Women in the Stories of the Apocryphal Acts.* Lewiston, N.Y.: E. Mellen Press, 1987 (Studies in Women and Religion 23).

Clark, Elizabeth A. *Ascetic Piety and Women's Faith: Essays on Late Ancient Christianity.* Lewiston, N.Y.: E. Mellen Press, 1986 (Studies in Women and Religion 20).

⸺. *Jerome, Chrysostom, and Friends: Essays and Translations.* New York: E. Mellen Press, 1979 (Studies in Women and Religion 1). Contains English translations of Chrysostom's "Life of Olympias" and "Treatises on the Subintroductae."

⸺. *Women in the Early Church.* Wilmington, Del.: Glazier, 1983 (Message of the Fathers of the Church 13).

Fiorenza, Elisabeth Schüssler. *In Memory of Her: A Feminist Theological Reconstruction of Christian Origins.* New York: Crossroad, 1985.

Gryson, Roger. *The Ministry of Women in the Early Church*. Collegeville, Minn.: Liturgical Press, 1976. Translation of *Le ministère des femmes dans l'Église ancienne*.

Heine, Susanne. *Women and Early Christianity: Are the Feminist Scholars Right?* London: SCM, 1987. Translation of *Frauen der frühen Christenheit*.

Laporte, Jean. *The Role of Women in Early Christianity*. New York: E. Mellen Press, 1982. (Studies in Women and Religion 7).

Massey, Les F. *Women and the New Testament: An Analysis of Scripture in Light of New Testament Era Culture*. Jefferson, N.C.: McFarland, 1989.

Portefaix, Lilian. *Sisters Rejoice: Paul's Letter to the Philippians and Luke-Acts as Seen by First-century Philippian Women*. Stockholm: Almqvist and Wiksell, 1988 (Coniectanea biblica New Testament series 20).

Salisbury, Joyce E. *Church Fathers, Independent Virgins*. London and New York: Verso, 1991.

Thurston, Bonnie Bowman. *The Widows: A Women's Ministry in the Early Church*. Philadelphia: Fortress Press, 1989.

Witherington, Ben. *Women in the Earliest Churches*. Cambridge and New York: Cambridge University Press, 1988.

Witherington, Ben, and Ann Witherington. *Women and the Genesis of Christianity*. New York: Cambridge University Press, 1990.

Works about Women in the Middle Ages

Adams, Carol. *From Workshop to Warfare: The Lives of Medieval Women*. New ed. Cambridge and New York: Cambridge University Press, 1990 (Women in History).

Bennett, Judith M. *Sisters and Workers in the Middle Ages*. Chicago: University of Chicago Press, 1989.

———. *Women in the Medieval English Countryside: Gender and Household in Brigstock before the Plague*. New York: Oxford University Press, 1987.

Berman, Constance H., Charles W. Connell, and Judith Rice Rothschild, eds. *The Worlds of Medieval Women: Creativity, Influence, Imagination*. Morgantown: West Virginia University Press, 1985 (Literary and Historical Perspectives of the Middle Ages 2).

Bloch, R. Howard. *Medieval Misogyny and the Invention of Western Romantic Love.* Chicago: University of Chicago Press, 1991.

Borst, Arno. *Die Katharer.* Stuttgart: Hiersemann, 1953 (Schriften der monumenta germaniae historica 12).

Bynum, Caroline Walker. *Fragmentation and Redemption: Essays on Gender and the Human Body in Medieval Religion.* New York: Zone Books, 1991.

———. *Holy Feast and Holy Fast: The Religious Significance of Food to Medieval Women.* Berkeley: University of California Press, 1987.

———. *Jesus as Mother: Studies in the Spirituality of the High Middle Ages.* Berkeley: University of California Press, 1982.

Classen, Albrecht. *Women as Protagonists and Poets in the German Middle Ages: An Anthology of Feminist Approaches to Middle High German Literature.* Göppingen: Kümmerle, 1991 (Göppinger Arbeiten zur Germanistik 528).

Dronke, Peter. *Women Writers of the Middle Ages: A Critical Study of Texts from Perpetua (d. 203) to Marguerite Porete (d. 1310).* Cambridge and New York: Cambridge University Press, 1984.

DuBruck, Edelgard E. *New Images of Medieval Women: Essays toward a Cultural Anthropology.* Lewiston, N.Y.: E. Mellen Press, 1989.

Ennen, Edith. *The Medieval Woman.* Oxford: Blackwell, 1989. Translation of *Frauen in Mittelalter.*

Fiero, Gloria K., Wendy Pfeffer, and Mathé Allain. *Three Medieval Views of Women: La Contenance des fames, Le Bien des fames, Le Blasme des fames.* New Haven: Yale University Press, 1989.

Gravdal, Kathryn. *Ravishing Maidens: Writing Rape in Medieval French Literature and Law.* Philadelphia: University of Pennsylvania Press, 1991 (New Cultural Studies series).

Holloway, Julia Bolton, Constance S. Wright, and Joan Bechtold. *Equally in God's Image: Women in the Middle Ages.* New York: P. Lang, 1990.

Howell, Martha C. *Women, Production, and Patriarchy in Late Medieval Cities.* Chicago: University of Chicago Press, 1986 (Women in Culture and Society).

Labarge, Margaret Wade. *Women in Medieval Life: A Small Sound of the Trumpet.* London: Hamish Hamilton, 1986.

Levin, Carole, and Jeanie Watson. *Ambiguous Realities: Women in the Middle Ages and Renaissance.* Detroit: Wayne State University Press, 1987.

Martin, Priscilla. *Chaucer's Women: Nuns, Wives, and Amazons.* Iowa City: University of Iowa Press, 1990.

McDonnell, Ernest W. *The Beguines and Beghards in Medieval Culture: With Special Emphasis on the Belgian Scene.* New Brunswick, N.J.: Rutgers University Press, 1954.

Mirrer, Louise. *Upon My Husband's Death: Widows in the Literature and Histories of Medieval Europe.* Ann Arbor: University of Michigan Press, 1992 (Studies in Medieval and Early Modern Civilization).

Mundy, John Hine. *Men and Women at Toulouse in the Age of the Cathars.* Toronto: Pontifical Institute of Mediaeval Studies, 1990.

Rose, Mary Beth. *Women in the Middle Ages and the Renaissance: Literary and Historical Perspectives.* Syracuse: Syracuse University Press, 1986.

Rosenthal, Joel Thomas. *Medieval Women and the Sources of Medieval History.* Athens: University of Georgia Press, 1990.

Stuard, Susan Mosher. *Women in Medieval History and Historiography.* Philadelphia: University of Pennsylvania Press, 1987.

Uitz, Erika. *The Legend of Good Women: Medieval Women in Towns and Cities.* Mount Kisco, N.Y.: Moyer Bell, 1990. Translation of *Die Frau in der mittelalterlichen Stadt.*

Beguines

Bowie, Fiona, ed., and Oliver Davies, trans. *Beguine Spirituality: Mystical Writings of Mechthild of Magdeburg, Beatrice of Nazareth, and Hadewijch of Brabant.* New York: Crossroad, 1990.

McDonnell, Ernest W. *The Beguines and Beghards in Medieval Culture: With Special Emphasis on the Belgian Scene.* New Brunswick, N.J.: Rutgers University Press, 1954.

McGinn, Bernard, ed. *Meister Eckhart and the Beguine Mystics: Hadewijch of Brabant, Mechtild of Magdeburg, and Marguerite Porete.* New York: Continuum, 1994.

McNamara, Jo Ann, John E. Halborg, and E. Gordon Whatley. *Sainted Women of the Dark Ages.* Durham, N.C.: Duke University Press, 1992.

Mirrer, Louise. *Upon My Husband's Death: Widows in the Literature and Histories of Medieval Europe.* Ann Arbor: University of Michigan Press, 1992 (Studies in Medieval and Early Modern Civilization).

Alphabetical Index

Chronological Index